THE NEW STUDENTS'
VEGGIE COOKBOOK

By Carolyn Humphries

foulsham
LONDON • NEW YORK • TORONTO • SYDNEY

foulsham

The Publishing House, Bennetts Close,
Cippenham, Slough, Berkshire, SL1 5AP, England

ISBN 0-572-02400-2

Illustrations by Sophie Azimont
Typeset by Grafica, Bournemouth.
Printed in Great Britain by Cox and Wyman Ltd, Reading

CONTENTS

FEED ME

INTRODUCTION

FEED ME

Leaving home for college or university is probably one of the biggest steps you'll take in life. Your first taste of real freedom where you are responsible for you – totally. The problem is, looking after yourself on a daily basis can be a bit of a drag if you don't get your act together. Thinking about shopping and cooking as well as enjoying a great social life (and, of course, studying) is a lot to cope with.

This book is designed for anyone who hasn't had to cook for themselves before. It won't insult you by telling you how to open a can of baked beans and put them on toast (mind you, that's a great standby) but it does have masses of really tasty, nourishing meals that don't cost a fortune, are dead simple and don't take ages to prepare. One of the pluses about being vegetarian is that you can often eat more cheaply than if you include meat in your diet. The book also has loads of advice on what to eat to keep fit and well and how to cook the basics – such as vegetables, pulses, pasta, rice and eggs. It has simple ways to make meals go further if you have friends round, food to eat to keep you going during exams and tasty snacks that can easily be turned into main meals to eke out the last few quid for the term. There's also a simple guide to what you'll need to buy, and basic food hygiene.

Eat well – eat wisely

To enjoy college life to the full (and to help the brain cells work) it is important to eat a healthy diet. That doesn't mean cranky food, just good, balanced meals. Remember try to eat:

- At least five portions of fruit and vegetables every day – any kind, any amount. You need them for vitamins, minerals and general well-being. Many are also cheap which helps a lot. Eat them cooked or raw, canned, frozen or fresh.

TIP: Market stalls are likely to be cheaper than the supermarket for fresh produce. If you are buying in a supermarket, look for economy ranges or buy loose rather than pre-packed – it's cheaper.

- Loads of starchy foods (carbohydrates) for energy and to fill you up. These are bread, potatoes, rice, pasta, breakfast cereals (wholegrain varieties such as muesli, porridge, Weetabix and Shredded Wheat rather than sugary ones such as Frosties or Cocopops). They're not fattening (it's the fat or sugary stuff you put on them that piles on weight).

TIP: Buy supermarket own brands. They're much cheaper.

- At least two portions of protein a day for body growth and repair. As you are not going to eat meat or fish, you must get yours from pulses (dried peas, beans and lentils, including baked beans), eggs, dairy products like cheese, milk and yoghurt (or soya alternatives if you are vegan), nuts and vegetable proteins like tofu or TVP (soya mince or chunks). I haven't used Quorn in the recipes because it's comparatively expensive and isn't approved by the Vegetarian Society because egg albumen from battery hens is used in its production.

- A very little fat – essential for body warmth and energy, BUT you don't need masses of extra butter or margarine or gallons of oil for frying. You get most of what you need naturally in other foods, such as dairy products, nuts and cereals, so have only a scraping of butter or marge on bread, use the minimum of oil for cooking (drain well before eating) and try to grill rather than fry foods where possible.

Equipment essentials

Most furnished accommodation supplies basic kitchen equipment which, hopefully, will include a cooker with an oven and a fridge with either a freezer or freezing compartment and basic crockery and cutlery but it's worth making sure you have the following:

★ Chopping board
★ Colander – for straining cooked vegetables etc.
★ Flameproof casserole (Dutch oven) with lid – a fairly small one which can be used on top of the stove or in the oven is useful
★ Bowls, at least one large for mixing and one pudding basin
★ Draining spoon, long-handled with holes in it
★ Fish slice
★ Frying pan (skillet)
★ Grater
★ Kettle
★ Kitchen scissors
★ Measuring jug, preferably with dry weights marked on it, too
★ Measuring spoons (not essential but better than guessing with ordinary cutlery)
★ Oven gloves
★ Ovenproof dish, medium-sized
★ Paperware – kitchen paper, foil and/or clingfilm (plastic wrap) and, ideally, greaseproof (waxed) paper
★ Pastry brush
★ Potato masher
★ Potato peeler
★ Rolling pin – not vital as a clean bottle will do instead

★ Roasting tins (baking pans), preferably one large and one small

★ Scales – not vital, especially if you have a measuring jug that shows dry weights

★ Sharp knives, at least one small and one large. A bread knife with a serrated edge is also useful

★ Saucepans, ideally one small, one medium and one large, with lids

★ Washing up cloths – packets of disposable ones are best although they can be shoved in the washing machine if times are hard!

★ Pan scourer – the green square ones are good but avoid those with sponge backs as you can never get rid of all the soap suds!

★ Tea towels (dish cloths) and hand towels

★ Whisk – a balloon one is ideal for making sauces etc.

★ Wooden spoon

The first big shopping list

Get all the basics you need at the beginning, then you'll just have to replace odds and ends each week as they run out.

Essential storecupboard items

★ Plain (all-purpose) and wholemeal flour

★ Baking powder

★ Bicarbonate of soda (baking soda) – it's not used in many recipes but is useful for other things: as a cure for indigestion – just 2.5 ml/½ tsp in some water; for freshening up the fridge – dissolve a little in some warm water and use to wipe out the inside of the fridge; for cleaning burnt saucepans – sprinkle some over the burnt bits, cover with warm water and leave to stand overnight

★ Salt

★ Pepper

★ Sugar – caster (superfine) is OK for most uses. Light brown is good too

★ Dried mixed herbs. These are essential, ideally plus dried basil, chives, mint and sage

- ★ Dried onion flakes and dried red and green (bell) peppers, not vital but great for brightening up rice or pasta and they keep for ages
- ★ Chilli powder
- ★ Cayenne
- ★ Curry powder or paste
- ★ Cinnamon and/or nutmeg
- ★ Ground ginger, not essential but useful, especially for Chinese-style dishes
- ★ Tube of tomato purée (paste)
- ★ Tube of garlic purée (paste), much easier than fiddling around crushing cloves
- ★ Vinegar, any sort. I use white or red wine vinegar but white distilled or malt are OK
- ★ Lemon juice, not vital but a bottle will keep in the fridge for ages and is better than vinegar in many recipes
- ★ Table sauces – ketchup (catsup), brown, Worcestershire and soy sauces
- ★ Oil – sunflower or good quality vegetable oil
- ★ Marmalade
- ★ Marmite (Vegemite) or other yeast extract, good as a drink made with boiling water as well as on toast and for flavouring. Highly nutritious, it's a good source of vitamin B12 which vegetarians are often deficient in
- ★ Mayonnaise or salad cream
- ★ Honey
- ★ Long-grain rice, white or brown
- ★ Pasta – quick-cook macaroni or other shapes, spaghetti, lasagne sheets, stuffed dried tortellini (you'll find it with the other pasta in supermarkets)
- ★ Dried pulses – split, marrowfat and chick peas (garbanzos), split red, whole green or brown lentils, various dried beans
- ★ Dried soya mince (TVP)
- ★ Instant mashed potato powder (useful)
- ★ Packet cheese sauce (not essential)
- ★ Packet sponge cake mix (useful)
- ★ Packet stuffing mix (useful)

★ Breakfast cereal. Choose a wholegrain one such as Weetabix, Shredded Wheat or muesli rather than a sweet sugary one – it'll fill you up for longer
★ Dried milk (non-fat dry milk), useful for cooking (not so good for drinking though OK in coffee or tea)

Canny Cans
★ Tomatoes – some brands of whole plum ones are incredibly cheap. Avoid well-known brands and ready-chopped ones
★ Baked beans
★ Other pulses – chick peas (garbanzos), lentils, haricot (navy), red kidney, cannellini, soya, mung, flageolet, butter and black-eyed beans, to name but a few!
★ Sweetcorn (corn)
★ Peas, carrots, green beans (useful to keep for some of the recipes and for quick accompaniments)
★ Condensed mushroom, celery and tomato soup (ideal for sauces)
★ Ratatouille
★ Any canned fruit – pineapple is very useful in cooking
★ Rice pudding
★ Custard

Perishables
★ Reduced fat spread (I've called it margarine in the recipes). Check the label to make sure it's suitable for spreading, cooking and for vegetarians, of course!
★ Medium eggs
★ Bread/rolls/pitta bread/naan – store in the feezer and take out when required. Sliced bread can be toasted from frozen if you forget to take it out in time
★ Cheese – choose a strong-flavoured one for cooking, then you don't need to use so much to get the right taste. Check the labels to make sure the cheese is suitable for vegetarians
★ Plain yoghurt – good for sauces and dressings, as well as for breakfast with cereal or with honey, or fruit for dessert

★ Milk – you can keep a carton in the freezer so you won't run out but it takes ages to thaw and will need a good shake once defrosted. Alternatively try long-life milk
★ Frozen peas/beans

Everyday fruit and veg
★ Apples
★ Oranges/satsumas/clementines
★ Bananas
★ Potatoes
★ Carrot
★ Onions
★ Salad stuffs (keep in the fridge)
★ Cabbage (especially white or savoy) is good shredded for salad as well as cooked

Basic Preparation

Whenever you read a cook book, it tells you to prepare various ingredients but it doesn't tell you how – until now:

Beat: Hold the bowl or pan in your left hand (or right if you are left-handed) and tilt slightly. Hold a wooden spoon in your other hand and stir the contents fast and firmly in one direction until smooth.

Chop: It's usually best to cut any vegetable or fruit in half first and put it cut side down on the chopping board. Then hold firmly in one hand and using a sharp knife make cuts at even distances along its length not quite through one end. Then, still holding it together, make cuts across it so it is cut into small pieces. To chop finely, simply make the cuts closer together. To chop coarsely, make them wider apart.

TIP: To chop fresh herbs, put them in a cup and snip with scissors for best results.

Dice: Much like chopping but in bigger cubes and you can cut right through the vegetable at both ends as it's easier to hold together.

Fold: Usually used when mixing a light, airy mixture. Use a metal spoon and gently cut and turn over the mixture using a figure-of-eight motion.

Grate: Hold the grater firmly in one hand over a plate and rub the ingredient to be grated up and down the appropriate side of the grater. To grate coarsely (usually for cheese, carrots, chocolate, etc), use the side with the largest holes. To grate finely (usually for lemon and other citrus rind), use the middle-sized holes, and for grating to a powder (for whole nutmeg) use the finest holes.

Knead: Usually of dough. Gently work the mixture together to a ball, then turn on to a board and squeeze and press the mixture until it forms a ball without any cracks.

Marinate: Coat vegetables, tofu, fruit or other ingredients in various flavourings and leave to stand for a while to allow the flavours to penetrate before cooking.

Mash: Use a potato masher or fork. Press the ingredient against the sides of the bowl or saucepan so it is forced through the gaps in the masher or fork to form a smoothish paste.

TIP: For potatoes, give them a good beat with the masher once mashed to make them fluffy.

Pare: Cut thin shreds of rind off something with a small sharp knife (serrated is often best).

Roll: Usually of pastry or other dough. Place the dough on a board, dusted with flour, and roll firmly but evenly with a rolling pin (or clean milk or wine bottle), always rolling away from you. Give the dough a quarter turn and repeat. Never roll from side to side as it stretches the dough which will then shrink on cooking.

Shred: cut into strips with a sharp knife. This is often used for lettuce or cabbage which can be cut down through the layers, then separated into strips.

Whip/whisk: Use a balloon whisk to beat the mixture in a circular motion, making sure you lift the mixture up with the whisk as you go to incorporate as much air as possible.

Basic cooking skills

The old chestnut 'He can't even boil an egg' isn't so funny – many people can't! Here are some simple instructions for all the basic foods you'll want to cook.

Eggs

Boiled: An egg pricker which you can buy in hardware shops is a great little gadget. You pierce the air sac end of the egg and it prevents it cracking when boiling. Place the egg(s) in a small saucepan and just cover with cold water. Cover with a lid (for quicker boiling) and bring to the boil. As soon as the water boils, start timing and cook for 4 minutes for runny yolks and firm whites, 5–6 minutes for hard-boiled.

TIP: For hard-boiled eggs to eat cold, plunge them immediately into cold water after cooking to prevent a black ring forming round the yolks.

Fried: Heat a very little oil in a frying pan (skillet). Break each egg into a cup and gently slide into the hot oil. Spoon the hot oil over the eggs as they fry and remove with a fish slice as soon as they are cooked to your liking.

Poached: Bring a frying pan (skillet) of water to simmering point and add 15 ml/1 tbsp vinegar or lemon juice. Break each egg into a cup and gently slide into the simmering water. Cook for 3 minutes for soft yolks, 4–5 minutes for hard. Do not allow to boil rapidly or the white will break up. Lift out with a fish slice.

Scrambled: Heat a knob of margarine and 15 ml/1 tbsp milk for each egg in a saucepan. Whisk in the eggs with a balloon whisk or fork. When well blended, add a little salt and pepper and cook over a gentle heat, stirring all the time, until the mixture scrambles but is creamy. Do not allow to boil or the mixture will go rubbery and watery. Serve immediately and soak the pan in hot soapy water straight away or it will be horrible to clean!

Omelette: Beat 2–3 eggs with 15 ml/1 tbsp water and a little salt and pepper. Heat a knob of margarine in a frying pan (skillet). Pour in the egg mixture and cook, lifting and stirring the egg until the base is golden and the egg is almost completely set. Tilt the pan, flip one third of the omelette over the centre, then fold again and slide out of the pan on to a warm plate, using a fish slice.

For a cheese omelette, add some slices of cheese to the omelette when almost set and continue cooking until the cheese melts.

Potatoes

Boiled: Peel or scrub and cut into even-sized pieces. Place in a pan with just enough cold water to cover. Add salt, if liked. Part-cover with a lid, bring to the boil, reduce the heat slightly and boil quickly until tender (about 10 minutes, depending on the size of the pieces). Drain and use as required.

Chipped: Peel, if liked, and cut each potato into finger-thick slices. Then cut each slice into chips. Pat dry on kitchen paper or in a clean tea towel (dish cloth). Heat enough oil to three-quarters-fill the frying pan (skillet) or at least 2.5 cm/1 in in a saucepan (or use a chip pan if you have one). To test the temperature, slide in one chip down the back of the fish slice into the oil. If it starts to sizzle immediately, the oil is ready. Gently slide the chips down the fish slice into the pan a handful at a time, and spread out with the slice. Cook until golden and soft in the centre. Don't add more chips than the pan will hold comfortably. If they are packed in and sticking out of the oil, the temperature will drop too much and they'll stew rather than fry crisply. Better to cook two batches if necessary. Drain on kitchen paper before serving.

Crispy potato skins: Scrub the potatoes, then peel fairly thickly. (Submerge the peeled potatoes in cold water to cook for the next meal.) Sprinkle a thin layer of salt on a baking sheet and lay the peelings on top. Bake in a preheated oven at 200°C/400°F/gas mark 6 for about 20 minutes until crispy. Toss and serve hot or cold. Alternatively, scrub the potatoes, cut in half lengthways and boil for about 10–15 minutes or until soft. Scoop out the potato into a bowl (mash and use for the next meal) leaving a thick 'shell' about 8 mm/⅜ in thick. Cut each shell into three or four wedges. Deep-fry as for chipped potatoes (see page 13) for 2–3 minutes until golden and crispy. Drain on kitchen paper, then season with salt and a dash of chilli powder if liked. Serve hot.

Jacket-baked: Scrub, leave whole and prick all over with a fork. Rub with oil and salt (if liked) and place directly on the middle shelf of the oven. Bake at 180°C/350°F/gas mark 4 for about 1 hour or until the potatoes feel soft when squeezed with an oven-gloved hand. The oven temperature isn't vital; cook longer in a slow oven or for less time in a hotter oven.

TIP: If you thread the potatoes on to metal skewers, they will cook more quickly as the heat is conducted through the centres.

Mashed: Prepare as for boiled but always peel first. Once boiled, strain off the water, then add a knob of margarine and a dash of milk. Mash with a potato masher or fork until smooth, then beat briefly until fluffy. Add a little more milk if the mixture looks too dry.

Roasted: Peel or scrub and cut into even-sized pieces. Place in a pan and just cover with water. Add a little salt, part-cover with a lid, bring to the boil and cook for 3–4 minutes. Drain off the water. Cover firmly with the lid and, holding the lid on, give the pan a really good shake to roughen the edges of the potatoes. Meanwhile, heat a little oil in a roasting tin (baking pan) in the oven until sizzling. Add the potatoes (careful – they will spit). Turn over in the oil, then roast at the top of the oven at 190°C/375°F/gas mark 5 for about 1 hour or until golden and crispy, turning once or twice.

Sautéed: Cut into small pieces or dice. Heat a little oil (or half margarine, half oil) in a frying pan (skillet) and fry, turning, until golden brown and cooked through – about 7 minutes, depending on the size. Add a little garlic towards the end of cooking, if liked. Drain on kitchen paper before serving.

Carrots and other root vegetables

Boiled: Peel or scrub, then slice or cut into fingers. Cook as for potatoes for 4–6 minutes or until tender.

Roasted: Prepare and cook as for potatoes, but there's no need to shake the pan after par-boiling.

Stir-fry: This doesn't just apply to roots but to any vegetables. Cut into even-sized matchsticks or slices. Heat a very little oil in a large frying pan or wok. Add the vegetables and toss, stirring until coated in oil and beginning to soften. Add any flavourings you like such as soy sauce, garlic, ginger and so on and continue cooking, stirring and tossing until just cooked but still with some 'bite'.

Green vegetables

Boiled: Shred or tear leafy ones, separate broccoli or cauliflower into small florets, top and tail beans or mangetout (snow peas), shell peas or broad (lima) beans. Drop into a very little boiling, lightly salted water, cover and boil rapidly until just tender, no longer. Drain (use the liquid for gravy or sauce if possible) and serve.

Steamed: Prepare as above but place in a colander over a pan of boiling water. Cover with a lid and steam until just tender. Don't put too many in the colander at one time and allow a little longer than boiling. Don't overcook or they will lose their colour and nutrients.

Rice

Boiled: Rinse and drain the rice. Bring a large pan of lightly salted water to the boil, add the rice, stir, then boil rapidly for 10–15 minutes until the rice is tender but the grains are still separate. Strain in a colander and pour some boiling water over to rinse off any excess starch and drain again.

TIP: If using the rice cold, pour cold water over it to cool it quickly.

Oven-baked: Use 1 part rice to 2½ parts salted water or stock. Melt a knob of margarine in a flameproof casserole (Dutch oven). Add the rice and stir to coat. Add the stock or water and bring to the boil. Cover and place in the oven at 180°C/350°F/gas mark 4. Cook for 20 minutes or until the rice is tender and has absorbed all the liquid.

Steamed: Use the same quantities as above. Rinse and place the rice in a pan. Cover with the liquid and bring just to the boil. Cover with a piece of foil, then a tight-fitting lid. Turn down the heat as low as possible and cook for 15 minutes. DO NOT UNCOVER. Turn off the heat and leave to stand for 5 minutes, then remove the cover and fluff up with a fork.

Pasta

Bring plenty of lightly salted water to the boil. Add the pasta and bring back to the boil. Add 15 ml/1 tbsp oil to prevent it boiling over, then boil rapidly for 10 minutes (or according to the packet directions), stirring occasionally to prevent sticking, until the pasta is just tender but still with a little 'bite'. Drain and use as required.

TIP: For spaghetti, bring the water to the boil, then stand the spaghetti in the water and gently push down so the spaghetti curls round in the pan as it softens in the boiling water.

Pulse

Most pulses, except split red lentils, need to be soaked well before cooking. Ideally place in a bowl and soal in cold water overnight. To speed up the process, use boiling water and leave for 2 hours.

When soaked, drain and place in a large saucepan of cold water. Do not add salt as this will toughen the skins. Bring to the boil and boil rapidly for 10 minutes. This is essential to destroy any toxins in the beans. Then reduce the heat, half-cover with a lid and simmer gently until tender. This can be anything from 1–3 hours depending on the variety. Drain and use as required.

TIP: To save fuel, cook a whole packet of pulses at a time, cool quickly and store in the fridge for several days or divide into quarters and freeze for use later. 100 g/4 oz/1½ cup dried pulses are equivalent to a 425 g/15 oz/large can.

Basic food hygiene

You may think some of the following are stating the obvious, but if you don't prepare, cook and store your food properly you're liable to get some pretty unpleasant side effects!

Preparing food

★ Always wash your hands before preparing food
★ Don't lick your fingers
★ Keep work surfaces and cooker clean and free from spills and debris
★ Don't use a cloth to wipe down a chopping board you've been cutting raw food on, for instance, then use the same one to wipe the surfaces – you'll simply spread germs. Always wash your cloth well in hot soapy water. Better still, use an anti-bacterial kitchen cleaner to wipe all surfaces
★ Always wash up in hot, soapy water and leave to drain, rather than dry up with a manky tea towel (dish cloth)
★ Keep the floor swept and washed or you may invite unwanted visitors such as mice to move in!
★ Don't leave dirty dishes festering in the kitchen (or elsewhere in the place!)
★ Empty the rubbish regularly

Storing food

★ Keep all perishables in the fridge
★ Any half-used contents of cans should always be transferred to a container with a lid, not left in the fridge in the can
★ Always cool leftovers quickly by transferring them from their hot cooking container into a clean cold one. Cover loosely and as soon as they're cold put them in the fridge, properly covered. But do wait until they're cold – hot food in the fridge raises the temperature and can make it unsafe for all the food in it
★ NEVER leave cooked food on the stove or in the oven overnight – the warm surroundings are the perfect breeding ground for bacteria

★ NEVER leave any food uncovered in the kitchen overnight. Any little 'friends' could have a snack while you're asleep (and I don't mean your flatmates!)

★ Always eat food by its use-by date (not the sell-by date). If you buy fresh food that is marked 'suitable for freezing' on its sell-by date but are not going to use it that day, freeze it immediately. When ready to cook it, make sure you thaw and use immediately. As soon as it is thawed, it is the same as it was the day you bought it. ALWAYS check the packaging to make sure food has not been previously frozen. If so, eat on the day of purchase

★ Don't keep cooked food festering in the fridge for days or weeks on end. As a rule of thumb, three or four days is about the limit for most things. Taste and smell are often a good guide to the state of your food. Anything that looks, smells or tastes off is off!

★ Don't refreeze foods that have defrosted unless you cook them first

Cooking properly

★ NEVER reheat foods more than once and ALWAYS make sure any reheated food is piping hot right through. Eat it lukewarm and you're asking for trouble

★ Check that prepared dishes are thoroughly cooked through before serving

★ With prepared frozen foods, check the packet directions to see if they should be cooked from frozen or thawed first

★ Don't keep tasting and stirring with the same spoon. I know they do it in the movies, but imagine all that slobber going to be dished out to everyone – UGH!

NOTES ON THE RECIPES

★ All ingredients are in metric, Imperial and American measures. Use only one set per recipe and don't mix them up

★ All eggs are medium unless otherwise stated

★ All spoon measures are level: 1 tsp = 5 ml, 1 tbsp = 15 ml

★ All can sizes are approximate – they differ slightly from brand to brand. For example, if I call for a 400 g/14 oz can of tomatoes, yours may be a 413 g can – that's fine

★ Wash and peel, if necessary, all fresh produce before using

★ All preparation and cooking times are approximate

★ Always preheat the oven and cook on the centre shelf unless otherwise stated

★ The recipes use dairy products. If you're vegan, omit these and use vegetarian alternatives, such as soya milk products. Make sure any cheese you use is suitable for vegetarians, too. Labels are usually clearly marked

★ Worcestershire sauce is a great flavour booster, but the traditional varieties include anchovies. So if you are seriously vegetarian, buy a brand from a health food shop

SNACKS AND LIGHT MEALS

FEED ME

You can always try a Marmite (Vegemite) and lettuce sandwich when you're peckish or good old beans on toast but it gets a bit boring after a while. Here's a range of tasty snacks that are very nutritious too and can just as easily be turned into main meals with extra salad, bread or spuds as appropriate (especially when you're trying to eke out the last few quid of the term).

TIP: If money is getting seriously low, remember that a bowl of wholegrain breakfast cereal with sliced banana or raisins and milk is a very nutritious meal and doesn't have to be just for breakfast.

Any of the following make good filling fodder:

★ Stuffed jacket potatoes: Bake them (see page 14), split in halves and scoop out the potato into a bowl. Mash with a little margarine and add any of the following: sweetcorn (corn) and grated cheese; baked beans and grated cheese and a splash of brown table sauce; chopped cucumber, nuts and mayonnaise; chopped tomato and grated cheese; yeast extract (ie Marmite (Vegemite)) and grated cheese; hard-boiled egg and mayonnaise; cottage cheese and chives or pineapple, peanut butter, chopped cucumber and mayonnaise.

★ Plain boiled pasta: Drain and add any of the following and cook gently, stirring until piping hot: a knob of margarine and lots of grated cheese; a can of chopped tomatoes with a few dried herbs and grated cheese; a drained can of peas, a knob of margarine and a little grated cheese; an egg beaten with a little milk, salt and pepper a few mixed herbs and/or garlic; an egg, beaten with a little milk, seasoning and a can of sweetcorn; some margarine, yeast extract (Marmite (Vegemite)) and grated cheese; peanut butter, a little milk and a pinch of chilli powder – cheese, too, if liked.

★ Plain boiled rice: Drain and add any of the following: a drained can of red kidney beans, some chilli powder and grated cheese; a drained can of peas, a beaten egg and some soy or Worcestershire sauce; a can of chopped tomatoes, some dried herbs and grated cheese; a drained can of pineapple, chick peas (garbanzos) and mayonnaise or soy sauce (good hot or cold).

Quick 'C' Snackwiches

Sandwiches are always useful but here are a few interesting ones which will bump up your vitamin C level.

★ Peanut butter and orange: Spread 1 slice of bread with peanut butter. Cover with thin slices of orange, cut across the segments. Season with a little pepper and top with a second slice of bread, thinly spread with margarine.

★ Soft cheese and orange: Prepare as above but use low-fat soft cheese instead of the peanut butter, spread on both slices of bread.

★ Pizza-style: Lightly spread 2 slices of bread with margarine. Cover 1 slice with grated Mozzarella or Cheddar cheese, top with slices of tomato and a sprinkling of dried basil, then add the second slice of bread.

★ Breakfast salad: Lightly spread 2 slices of bread with margarine. Spread cottage cheese with pineapple over 1 slice. Spread a little orange marmalade over the other and sandwich together.

★ Banana bite: Lightly spread 2 slices of bread with low-fat soft cheese or margarine. Mash a banana and spread over 1 slice. Top with a segmented satsuma or clementine and then add the other slice of bread.

★ Christmas-style: Spread 2 slices of bread lightly with margarine. Spread 1 slice with vegetarian mincemeat and top with a slice of strong Cheddar cheese, then sandwich together with the other slice of bread.

★ Thai-style: Spread 1 slice of bread with peanut butter. Sprinkle with chilli powder and top with some fresh bean sprouts and a drained chopped ring of canned pineapple. (Add the rest of the pineapple to any of the stir-fries in this book or serve with plain yoghurt for dessert.) Sprinkle lightly with soy sauce and sandwich together with a second slice of bread lightly spread with margarine.

EGGY BREAD

Serves 1–2

Ingredients	Metric	Imperial	American
Eggs	2	2	2
Milk	15 ml	1 tbsp	1 tbsp
Salt and pepper			
Slices of bread	4	4	4
Oil for frying			

1. Beat the eggs and milk together in a shallow dish with a little salt and pepper.

2. Cut the slices of bread in half and dip in the egg and milk until completely soaked.

3. Heat a little oil in a frying pan (skillet) and fry (sauté) the bread on each side until golden brown.

4. Sprinkle with a little salt and serve straight away.

Preparation time: 2 minutes
Cooking time: 5 minutes

SIMPLE SWEETCORN CHOWDER

Serves 4

Ingredients	Metric	Imperial	American
Onion, chopped	1	1	1
Potatoes, thinly sliced	450 g	1 lb	1 lb
Can of sweetcorn (corn)	350 g	12 oz	1 large
Vegetable stock, made with 2 stock cubes	750 ml	1¼ pts	3 cups
Salt and pepper			
Milk	150 ml	¼ pt	⅔ cup

I. Put all the ingredients except the milk in a saucepan. Bring to the boil, reduce the heat, part-cover and simmer for 30 minutes or until the potatoes are really soft.

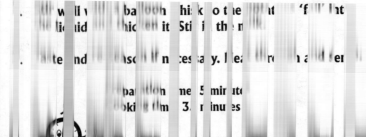

SPECIAL TIFFIN

Serves 2 or 4

Ingredients	Metric	Imperial	American
Naan breads	2	2	2
Can of pease pudding	225 g	8 oz	1 small
Curry paste or powder	10 ml	2 tsp	2 tsp
Mango chutney or sweet pickle	30 ml	2 tbsp	2 tbsp
Lemon juice (optional)			
Thinly sliced cucumber			
Finely chopped onion			

1. **Grill (broil) the naans as directed on the packet.**

2. **Meanwhile, heat the pease pudding in a saucepan and stir in the curry paste or powder and chutney or pickle.**

3. **Spread over the breads, sprinkle with a little lemon juice (if using), then top with slices of cucumber and some finely chopped onion. Fold in half, cut each into 4 wedges and hold in a piece of kitchen paper to eat.**

Preparation time: 5 minutes
Cooking time: 5 minutes

CHEESE AND TOMATO BAGEL PIZZA

Serves 1

Ingredients	Metric	Imperial	American
Bagel	1	1	1
Margarine for spreading			
A little tomato purée (paste)			
Cheddar cheese, grated	25 g	1 oz	¼ cup
Tomato, sliced	1	1	1
Good pinch of dried mixed herbs or basil			

1. Cut the bagel in half and toast under a hot grill (broiler). Spread thinly with margarine, then the tomato purée. Top with some grated cheese and sliced tomato and sprinkle with the herbs. Grill (broil) until the cheese melts and bubbles.

Preparation time: nil
Cooking time: 10 minutes

CREAMY MUSHROOM CROISSANTS

Serves 1 or 2

Ingredients	Metric	Imperial	American
Croissants	2 large or 4 small	2 large or 4 small	2 large or 4 small
Can of creamed mushrooms	215 g	7½ oz	1 small

1. Split the croissants through the middle but not completely, to form a pocket in each.

2. Spread the creamed mushrooms inside.

3. Place under a moderate grill (broiler), not too near the heat source, for about 2 minutes on each side until piping hot through. Take care not to let the croissants burn.

Preparation time: 5 minutes
Cooking time: 4 minutes

WAFFLE A LOT

Serves 1–2

Ingredients	Metric	Imperial	American
Potato waffles	2	2	2
Slices of Cheddar cheese	2	2	2
Eggs	2	2	2
A little oil			
Shredded lettuce			
Mayonnaise			

1. Grill (broil) the waffles according to the packet directions.

2. Top each with a slice of cheese and return to the grill until melted.

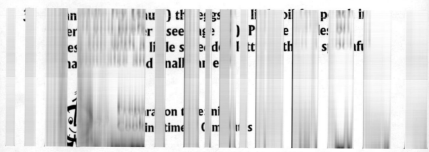

RUSSIAN SALAD PITTAS

Serves 1–2

Ingredients	Metric	Imperial	American
Pitta breads	2	2	2
Can of diced mixed vegetables, drained	275 g	10 oz	1 small
Mayonnaise	30 ml	2 tbsp	2 tbsp
Salt and pepper			
Shredded lettuce			

1. Split the pitta breads along one side and open up to form pockets.

2. Mix the vegetables with the mayonnaise and a little salt and pepper.

3. Spoon into the pitta breads and add a little shredded lettuce.

 Preparation time: 5 minutes

FRENCH-STYLE PITTA

Serves 1

Ingredients	Metric	Imperial	American
Egg	1	1	1
Milk	15 ml	1 tbsp	1 tbsp
Dried mixed herbs	1.5 ml	¼ tsp	¼ tsp
Salt and pepper			
Knob of margarine			
Pitta breads	1 or 2	1 or 2	1 or 2
Shredded lettuce			
Mayonnaise			

1. Beat the egg with the milk, herbs and a little salt and pepper.

2. Heat the margarine in a small frying pan (skillet) and fry

3.

Cooking time: 5 minutes

HOT PLOUGHMAN'S

An ordinary Ploughman's – bread, cheese, a tomato and a
pickled onion or some sweet pickle – makes a great,
nutritious meal on a warm day. Here's a version for
all those other days!

Serves 4

Ingredients	Metric	Imperial	American
Small uncut loaf	1	1	1
Margarine for spreading			
Cheddar cheese, sliced	225 g	8 oz	2 cups
Sweet pickle			
To serve: Tomatoes			

1. Cut the loaf into thick slices but not right through the
   base so each slice is still attached. Spread with a little
   margarine between each cut.

2. Put a slice of cheese and a spoonful of pickle between
   each slice, then wrap the whole thing in foil.

3. Bake in a preheated oven at 220°C/425°F/gas mark 7 for
   15–20 minutes until the crust is crisp and the cheese has
   melted.

4. Serve with tomatoes (and pickled onions if you like!).

Preparation time: 5 minutes
Cooking time: 20 minutes

FRENCH CHEESE LOAF

Another way to 'show off' rather than dish up the mundane.

Serves 4

Ingredients	Metric	Imperial	American
French stick	1	1	1
Margarine for spreading			
Round Camembert, thinly sliced	1	1	1
Tomatoes, sliced	3	3	3
Dried mixed herbs			

1. Cut the French stick into slices but not right through the base.

2. Spread with a little margarine between each slice.

3. Add a slice of Camembert and tomato, sprinkled with herbs, between each slice.

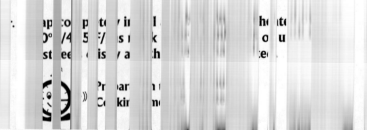

GARLIC BREAD

This is great on its own with a hunk of cheese and some salad or served with any soup or main course.

Serves 4

Ingredients	Metric	Imperial	American
Soft margarine	100 g	4 oz	½ cup
Garlic purée (paste)	5 ml	1 tsp	1 tsp
Dried mixed herbs (optional)	5 ml	1 tsp	1 tsp
Small French stick	1	1	1

1. Mash together the margarine, garlic purée and herbs, if using.

2. Cut the French stick in slices, not quite through the base, then spread the garlic mixture between each slice and over the top.

3. Wrap in foil and bake in a preheated oven at 200°C/400°F/gas mark 6 for about 15 minutes until the crust feels crisp and the centre is soft.

Preparation time: 5–10 minutes
Cooking time: 15 minutes

EGGY CORN WAFFLE WEDGES

Serves 2

Ingredients	Metric	Imperial	American
Small banana, thickly sliced	1	1	1
Margarine for frying			
Eggs	2	2	2
Water	15 ml	1 tbsp	1 tbsp
Can of sweetcorn (corn)	200 g	7 oz	1 small
Salt and pepper			
Knob of margarine			
Bought waffles	2	2	2

1. Fry (sauté) the banana slices in a little margarine in a frying pan (skillet) for 1 minute. Remove from the pan.

2. [text obscured] water [text obscured] of [text obscured] ta[text obscured].

3. M[text obscured]lt [text obscured]k [text obscured] ri[text obscured] in [text obscured]ir [text obscured]pa[text obscured]p[text obscured] in [text obscured]h[text obscured] eg[text obscured] [text obscured]tu[text obscured]. F[text obscured]ng [text obscured]rig [text obscured]til [text obscured] a[text obscured] [text obscured]u de[text obscured]

4. S[text obscured]t[text obscured]r [text obscured]ic[text obscured] ov[text obscured] [text obscured]p [text obscured]ng [text obscured]g[text obscured] [text obscured]u[text obscured]de[text obscured] a [text obscured]il[text obscured]) b[text obscured] [text obscured]o [text obscured]w[text obscured] t[text obscured] Pu[text obscured] the waffles on the grill pan at the same time [text obscured] w[text obscured]h.

5. Put the waffles on plates. Fold the corn omelette in half, then cut in half to form 2 wedges. Put one on each waffle and serve.

Preparation time: 5 minutes
Cooking time: 10 minutes

VEGETABLE-BASED DISHES

FEED ME

Nothing is etched in stone so ring the changes with different vegetables that take your fancy (or particularly cheap at the time!). As a rough guide, you can substitute any root vegetable for another, any green vegetable for another and so on. Make sure you cut them up to a similar size so they cook in roughly the same time.

Many of the recipes serve two or three people – enough for two days for one person. Double the quantities if you're cooking for flatmates or friends.

PEASANT SOUP

Serves 4

Ingredients	Metric	Imperial	American
Can of tomatoes	400 g	14 oz	1 large
Onion, chopped	1	1	1
Large carrot, chopped	1	1	1
Large potato, chopped	1	1	1
Small cabbage, shredded	¼	¼	¼
Vegetable stock, made with 2 stock cubes	750 ml	1¼ pts	3 cups
Can of haricot (navy) beans, drained	425 g	15 oz	1 large
Dried mixed herbs	5 ml	1 tsp	1 tsp
Salt and pepper			

To serve: Pecorino or Cheddar cheese, grated

1. Empty the tomatoes into a large pan and break up wh... wooden spoon.

2. Add the remaining ingredients, bring to the boil, reduce the heat, part-cover and simmer for 20–30 minutes until all the vegetables are really ... Taste and re-season if necessary.

3. **Serve sprinkled with grated cheese.**

Preparation time: 10 minutes
Cooking time: 30 minutes

FRENCH ONION SOUP

Serves 4

Ingredients	Metric	Imperial	American
Large onions, roughly chopped	4	4	4
Light brown sugar	10 ml	2 tsp	2 tsp
Vegetable stock, made with 2 stock cubes	900 ml	1½ pts	3¾ cups
Salt and pepper			
Slices of French bread	4	4	4
Cheddar cheese, grated	100 g	4 oz	1 cup

1. Melt the margarine in a saucepan and fry (sauté) the onions for 5 minutes, stirring, until turning golden.

2. Add the sugar and continue frying for 3–4 minutes until a rich golden brown, stirring all the time.

3. Stir in the stock and a little salt and pepper, bring to the boil, reduce the heat, part-cover and simmer gently for 15–20 minutes until the onions are really soft. Taste and re-season if necessary.

4. When ready to serve, toast the bread on both sides. Place in soup bowls and top with the cheese. Spoon the soup over and serve.

Preparation time: 5 minutes
Cooking time: 30 minutes

CURRIED PARSNIP AND POTATO SOUP

You can substitute carrots instead for the parsnips and potatoes if you prefer. If you've got any leftover cooked rice, throw it in before reheating at the end for an even more filling meal.

Serves 4

Ingredients	Metric	Imperial	American
Large parsnips, sliced	2	2	2
Large potatoes, sliced	2	2	2
Onion, chopped	1	1	1
Vegetable stock, made with 2 stock cubes	750 ml	1¼ pts	3 cups
Curry powder or paste	5 ml	1 tsp	1 tsp
Salt and pepper			
A little milk			

1. ... ingredients except the ... sa... pan. ...e ..l, reduce the hea... p... co...ve... l sim...er ... 1... in...tes or u...til th... ve...ab...es ... reall...

2. ... th... ...oc... into a ...owl. ...la... the ve...ables well, then sti... in the stock again. Th... ...wi...h ...le mi...k if liked.

3. Taste and re-season if necessary. Reheat and serve with naan bread.

Preparation time: 5 minutes
Cooking time: 20 minutes

SMOOTH PEANUT SOUP

Serves 4

Ingredients	Metric	Imperial	American
Small onion	1	1	1
Knob of margarine			
Plain (all-purpose) flour	15 ml	1 tbsp	1 tbsp
Vegetable stock, made with 2 stock cubes	750 ml	1¼ pts	3 cups
Smooth peanut butter	225 g	8 oz	1 cup
Milk	150 ml	¼ pt	⅔ cup
Salt and pepper			
Slices of bread	4	4	4
Cheddar cheese, sliced	75 g	3 oz	¾ cup

I. **Grate the onion straight into a saucepan. Add the knob of margarine and fry (sauté), stirring for 30 seconds. Stir in the flour.**

2. **Remove from the heat and gradually blend in the stock, stirring all the time.**

3. **Bring to the boil, stirring, then blend in the peanut butter, stirring until it has melted.**

4. **Stir in the milk and season to taste. Heat through.**

5. **Meanwhile, toast the bread on both sides. Cover with slices of cheese and grill (broil) until the cheese has melted. Cut into pieces and serve with the soup.**

Preparation time: 5 minutes
Cooking time: 10 minutes

ALMOST INSTANT VEGETABLE GRILL

Serves 2–3

Ingredients	Metric	Imperial	American
Knob of margarine			
Oil	15 ml	1 tbsp	1 tbsp
Can of new potatoes, drained	500 g	1 lb 2 oz	1 large
Frozen mixed vegetables, thawed	225 g	8 oz	1 pkt
Plain yoghurt	150 ml	¼ pt	⅔ cup
Mayonnaise	15 ml	1 tbsp	1 tbsp
Salt and pepper			
Cheddar cheese, grated	50 g	2 oz	½ cup

1. Heat the margarine and oil in a flameproof casserole (Dutch oven). Add all the vegetables and fry (sauté), stirring, for 5 minutes.

2. Stir in the yogurt, mayonnaise and a little salt and pepper. Cook over a gentle heat for 3–4 minutes, stirring occasionally. Do not allow to boil.

3. Sprinkle with the cheese and place under a hot grill (broiler) until the cheese melts.

4. Serve straight from the pan.

Preparation time: 5 minutes plus thawing
Cooking time: about 12 minutes

WALDORF STEW

Serves 2

Ingredients	Metric	Imperial	American
French (green) beans, topped and tailed and cut in 2 or 3 pieces	100 g	4 oz	4 oz
Vegetable stock, made with ½ stock cube	150 ml	¼ pt	⅔ cup
Can of sweetcorn (corn)	200 g	7 oz	1 small
Small onion, thinly sliced	1	1	1
Tomatoes, quartered	2	2	2
Small eating (dessert) apple, chopped	1	1	1
Walnuts, roughly chopped	40 g	1½ oz	⅓ cup
Salt and pepper			
To serve: Crusty bread			

I. **Simmer the beans and stock in a covered pan for 7 minutes.**

2. **Add the can of sweetcorn with its liquid and all the remaining ingredients. Bring to the boil, reduce the heat, part-cover and simmer for 5 minutes, stirring occasionally.**

3. **Taste and re-season if necessary. Serve with crusty bread.**

Preparation time: 10 minutes
Cooking time: 15 minutes

ROOT SATAY

Serves 2–3

Ingredients	Metric	Imperial	American
Turnip, cut into bite-sized chunks	1	1	1
Large carrot, cut into bite-sized chunks	1	1	1
Parsnip, cut into bite-sized chunks	1	1	1
Small swede (rutabaga), cut into bite-sized chunks	1	1	1
Knob of margarine			
Honey	15 ml	1 tbsp	1 tbsp
For the sauce:			
Peanut butter	75 ml	5 tbsp	5 tbsp
Milk	150 ml	¼ pt	⅔ cup
illi wd	2.5 ml	sp	½ t
lt a pe er			
se : B led ice ge 5–16)			

C ok l t v les n boilin lig tly l d v er
u til j st n in, inse wi co l wa er nd ai
a in

2. **Thread alternately on kebab skewers. Lay on foil on a grill (broiler) rack.**

3. **Melt the margarine and honey together and brush over the kebabs. Grill (broil), turning occasionally, until lightly golden, brushing with the margarine and honey mixture.**

4. Meanwhile, put the sauce ingredients in a saucepan and heat through, stirring.

5. Serve the kebabs on a bed of boiled rice with the sauce spooned over.

 Preparation time: 15 minutes
Cooking time: 20 minutes

INSTANT RATATOUILLE SUPPER

Serves 2

Ingredients	Metric	Imperial	American
Servings of instant mashed potato	2	2	2
Knob of margarine			
Can of ratatouille	425 g	15 oz	1 large
Cheddar cheese, grated	50 g	2 oz	½ cup

I. Make up the potato according to packet directions and spoon round the edge of 2 individual flameproof dishes (or dinner plates). Dot with margarine and grill (broil) until turning brown.

2. Meanwhile, heat the ratatouille in a saucepan until piping hot. Spoon in to the centre of the potato and sprinkle with cheese. Return to the grill for a few moments to melt the cheese, if liked.

 Preparation time: 5 minutes
Cooking time: 5 minutes

FRENCH PEA BREAD

Serves 2

Ingredients	Metric	Imperial	American
Frozen peas	50 g	2 oz	½ cup
Small egg, beaten	1	1	1
Mayonnaise	15 ml	1 tbsp	1 tbsp
Spring onion (scallion) or a small onion, finely chopped (optional)	1	1	1
Small French stick, split in half lengthways	1	1	1
Margarine	25 g	1 oz	2 tbsp
Garlic purée (paste)	2.5 ml	½ tsp	½ tsp
Dried mint or mixed herbs	2.5 ml	½ tsp	½ tsp
Cheddar cheese, grated	50 g	2 oz	½ cup

Cook the peas in ti h ter for **10 minutes.** Drain and mash

Mix in the beat   an onion, if using.

Toast the Fren   d

Mash the marg   g   puée and mint. Spread on the cut side of the French bread. Top with the pea mixture and then the grated cheese. Grill (broil) until set and golden.

Preparation time: 12–15 minutes
Cooking time: 5 minutes

MUSHROOM STROGANOFF

Serves 2

Ingredients	Metric	Imperial	American
Margarine	40 g	1½ oz	3 tbsp
Small onion, chopped	1	1	1
Garlic purée (paste)	5 ml	1 tsp	1 tsp
Mushrooms, quartered	750 g	1½ lb	1½ lb
White wine or cider	75 ml	5 tbsp	5 tbsp
Cornflour (cornstarch)	7.5 ml	1½ tsp	1½ tsp
Soured (dairy sour) cream or plain yoghurt	150 ml	¼ pt	⅔ cup
Salt and pepper			

To serve: Plain boiled rice (see page 15–16) OR tagliatelle and a few dried chives or a little fresh chopped parsley (optional)

1. Melt the margarine in a large pan and fry (sauté) the onion and garlic purée for 2 minutes, stirring.

2. Add the mushrooms, cover and cook gently for 10 minutes. Remove the lid and continue cooking until all the liquid has evaporated, stirring occasionally.

3. Add the wine or cider and simmer for 5 minutes.

4. Blend the cornflour with a little water and stir into the pan with the cream or yoghurt. Simmer, stirring, for 4 minutes until thickened.

5. Season to taste and serve sprinkled with chives or parsley, if liked, on a bed of rice or pasta.

Preparation time: 5 minutes
Cooking time: 20–25 minutes

AS EASY AS VEGETABLE PIE!

You can always use ready-made fresh or frozen pastry,
but making your own is really easy – and cheaper!

Serves 4

Ingredients	Metric	Imperial	American
For the pastry (paste):			
Plain (all-purpose) flour	225 g	8 oz	2 cups
Pinch of salt			
Soft margarine	100 g	4 oz	½ cup
Cold water	60 ml	4 tbsp	4 tbsp
For the filling:			
Frozen mixed vegetables, thawed	175 g	6 oz	1½ cups
Can of cream of mushroom soup	400 g	14 oz	1 large
Dried mixed herbs	5 ml	1 tsp	1 tsp
Pepper			
A little milk			

1. Make the pastry. Put the flour and salt in a bowl and add the margarine. Using a fork, 'mash' the margarine into the flour until the mixture looks like breadcrumbs.

2. Mix with enough of the water to form a firm dough.

3. Dust a little flour over the work surface and knead the dough into a ball. Cut the dough in half and roll out one half and use to line a shallow pie dish (or even an ovenproof dinner plate).

4. To make the filling, mix the vegetables with the soup, mixed herbs and a little pepper. Spoon into the centre of the pastry.

5. Roll out the rest of the pastry to a round big enough to cover the pie. Brush the pastry edge with water and put the lid in position. Trim the edges with a knife to fit, if necessary. Press the edges all round with a fork to seal the top and bottom layers together. Make a small slit in the centre to let the steam escape and brush all over with milk to glaze.

6. Stand the pie on a baking sheet if you have one (it helps cook the pastry base), then bake in a preheated oven at 200°C/400°F/gas mark 6 for 30 minutes until golden brown.

Preparation time: 15 minutes
Cooking time: 30 minutes

SWEET AND SOUR STIR-FRY

Serves 2

Ingredients	Metric	Imperial	American
Oil	15 ml	1 tbsp	1 tbsp
Small onion, sliced	1	1	1
Small red or green (bell) pepper, sliced	1	1	1
Cucumber, cut into matchsticks	¼	¼	¼
Carrot, cut into matchsticks	1	1	1
Can of pineapple chunks in natural juice	300 g	11 oz	1 small
Tomato ketchup (catsup)	15 ml	1 tbsp	1 tbsp
Soy sauce	15 ml	1 tbsp	1 tbsp
Vinegar	15 ml	1 tbsp	1 tbsp
Honey	10 ml	2 tsp	2 tsp
Cornflour (cornstarch)	7.5 ml	1½ tsp	1½ tsp
Water	30 ml	2 tbsp	2 tbsp
Bean sprouts	100 g	4 oz	4 oz
To serve: Boiled rice (see page 15–16) OR Chinese egg noodles			

1. Heat the oil in a wok or large frying pan (skillet). Add the vegetables and stir-fry for 4 minutes.

2. Drain the pineapple juice into a bowl, reserving the fruit, then blend in the remaining ingredients except the bean sprouts.

3. Add to the stir-fried vegetables and simmer for 2 minutes, stirring. Add the reserved pineapple and bean sprouts and heat through, stirring for 2 minutes.

4. Serve with boiled rice or Chinese egg noodles.

Preparation time: 5 minutes
Cooking time: 8 minutes

VEGETABLE CRUMBLE

Serves 3–4

Ingredients	Metric	Imperial	American
Oil	30 ml	2 tbsp	2 tbsp
Red (bell) pepper, sliced	1	1	1
Courgettes (zucchini), sliced	450 g	1 lb	1 lb
Mushrooms, sliced	100 g	4 oz	4 oz
Can of tomatoes	400 g	14 oz	1 large
Garlic purée (paste)	5 ml	1 tsp	1 tsp
Pepper			
Dried basil or mixed herbs	2.5 ml	½ tsp	½ tsp
Cheddar cheese, grated	175 g	6 oz	1½ cups
Slices of wholemeal bread, crumbled	3	3	3

1. Heat the oil in a flameproof casserole (Dutch oven) and fry (sauté) the pepper, courgettes and mushrooms for about 3 minutes, stirring, until slightly softened.

2. Add the tomatoes and break up with a wooden spoon. Stir in the remaining ingredients except the cheese and breadcrumbs. Reduce the heat, cover and simmer for 0 minutes, stirring occasionally.

3. Mix together the cheese and breadcrumbs and sprinkle over the top. Bake in a preheated oven at 200°C/400°F/gas mark 6 for about 25 minutes until turning golden on top.

Preparation time: 5 minutes
Cooking time: about 40 minutes

VEGGIE-STUFFED LEAVES

Serves 2–4

Ingredients	Metric	Imperial	American
Large outside cabbage leaves	4	4	4
Vegetable stock, made with 1 stock cube	300 ml	½ pt	1¼ cups
Packet of vegetarian burger mix	100 g	4 oz	1 small
Oil	45 ml	3 tbsp	3 tbsp
Small onion, finely chopped	1	1	1
Tomato purée (paste)	15 ml	1 tbsp	1 tbsp

To serve: Mashed potato (see page 14)

1. Trim any thick stalk from the centre of the cabbage leaves. Rinse well and place in a shallow pan with the stock. Bring to the boil, cover and simmer for 3 minutes until slightly softened. Remove from the stock and lay the leaves side by side on a chopping board.
2. Reconstitute the burger mix according to the packet directions.
3. Heat 30 ml/2 tbsp of the oil in a pan and fry (sauté) the onion for 2 minutes. Add the oil and onion to the burger mix with the tomato purée and mix well.
4. Divide between the cabbage leaves. Fold over the 2 sides, then roll up to form parcels – a bit like spring rolls. Lay, folded sides down, in the stock in the pan. Bring to the boil, cover and simmer for about 5 minutes until cooked through and piping hot.
5. Serve with mashed potatoes and pour the hot stock over them.

Preparation time: 5 minutes
Cooking time: 15 minutes

CURRIED POTATO NESTS

For speed I've suggested using instant mashed potato, but
you can use the real thing if you prefer. 3 or 4 potatoes
should be sufficient. Simply flavour with the curry
powder and tomato purée after mashing with some
milk and margarine.

Serves 2–3

Ingredients	Metric	Imperial	American
Packet of frozen mixed vegetables	225 g	8 oz	1 small
Water	300 ml	½ pt	1¼ cups
Milk	175 ml	6 fl oz	¾ cup
Tomato purée (paste)	5 ml	1 tsp	1 tsp
Knob of margarine			
Curry powder or paste	2.5 ml	½ tsp	½ tsp
Instant mashed potato powder or granules	150 g	5 oz	1 large pkt
Cheddar cheese, grated	50 g	2 oz	½ cup

1. Cook the vegetables according to the packet directions.
   Drain.

2. Meanwhile, heat the water and milk together in a
   saucepan. Add the tomato purée, margarine and curry
   powder or paste and mix until well blended. Use to
   reconstitute the potato.

3. Spoon in a ring on 2 serving plates. Spoon the hot
   vegetables into the centre and sprinkle with the grated
   cheese before serving.

Preparation time: nil
Cooking time: 10 minutes

THE DAY-AFTER PIE

Serves 2–3

Ingredients	Metric	Imperial	American
Cooked, leftover vegetables, chopped (or use frozen, cooked, if you prefer)	225 g	8 oz	8 oz
Can of baked beans	400 g	14 oz	1 large
Slices of bread, crumbled	3	3	3
Marmite (Vegemite)	10 ml	2 tsp	2 tsp
Boiling water	30 ml	2 tbsp	2 tbsp
Dried mixed herbs	2.5 ml	½ tsp	½ tsp
Salt and pepper			
Potatoes, boiled and mashed (see page 14)	450 g	1 lb	1 lb
Knob of margarine			

1. Mix the vegetables with the beans and bread in an ovenproof dish.

2. Blend the Marmite with the water and stir in with the herbs and a little salt and pepper.

3. Spread the mashed potatoes on top and dot with margarine.

4. Bake in a preheated oven at 220°C/425°F/gas mark 7 for about 30 minutes until golden brown and piping hot.

Preparation time: 20 minutes
Cooking time: 30 minutes

VEGETABLE CURRY

Throw in a handful of raisins or sultanas (golden raisins),
if you have any, and serve slices of banana or apple
as a tasty side dish.

Serves 2–3

Ingredients	Metric	Imperial	American
Potatoes, diced	2	2	2
Carrots, diced	2	2	2
Small cauliflower, cut into florets	1	1	1
Oil	15 ml	1 tbsp	1 tbsp
Onion, chopped	1	1	1
Curry powder	15 ml	1 tbsp	1 tbsp
Tomato purée (paste)	15 ml	1 tbsp	1 tbsp
Garlic purée (paste)	2.5 ml	½ tsp	½ tsp
Frozen peas	50 g	2 oz	½ cup
Desiccated (shredded) coconut	30 ml	2 tbsp	2 tbsp
OR block of creamed coconut, cut into small pieces	¼	¼	¼
Lemon juice	10 ml	2 tsp	2 tsp
Salt and pepper			
To serve: Boiled rice (see page 15–16)			

1. Cook the potatoes, carrots and cauliflower in boiling,
   salted water for 5 minutes. Drain, reserving the cooking
   water.

2. Meanwhile, heat the oil in a separate saucepan and fry (sauté) the onion, stirring, for 2 minutes. Add the remaining ingredients except the salt and pepper with enough of the reserved cooking water to make a thickish sauce. Stir until the creamed coconut, if using, has dissolved, then season to taste.

3. Add the part-cooked vegetables, stir gently, then cover and simmer over a gentle heat, stirring occasionally, until the vegetables are just tender and bathed in a rich sauce. Thin with a little more of the cooking water if necessary.

4. Serve on a bed of boiled rice.

Preparation time: 5 minutes
Cooking time: about 25 minutes

TABBOULEH

A trendy and highly nutritious dish from the Middle East.
Jazz it up with a handful of chopped nuts, pine nuts,
pumpkin or sunflower seeds, or a few sliced olives.
If you invest in a bag of fresh parsley for this, put the rest
in the freezer and use, chopped, to garnish any dish or to
add flavour.

Serves 4

Ingredients	Metric	Imperial	American
Bulgar wheat	175 g	6 oz	1½ cups
Boiling water	325 ml	11 fl oz	1⅓ cups
Salt	5 ml	1 tsp	1 tsp
Oil	45 ml	3 tbsp	3 tbsp
Lemon juice or vinegar	45 ml	3 tbsp	3 tbsp
Garlic purée (paste)	5 ml	1 tsp	1 tsp
Chopped fresh parsley (it's worth it in this!)	30 ml	2 tbsp	2 tbsp
Dried mint	5 ml	1 tsp	1 tsp
Pepper			
Tomatoes, chopped	4		4
Cucumber, chopped	¼		¼
Small onion, sliced and separated into rings	1		1

1. Put the wheat in a bowl and pour over the boiling water.
   Sprinkle with the salt, stir and leave to stand for
   20 minutes until the wheat has absorbed all the liquid.

2. Drizzle over the oil and lemon juice or vinegar, the herbs
   and some pepper. Mix well, leave to cool, then chill, in
   the refrigerator.

3. Just before serving, stir in the tomatoes and cucumber and scatter the onion rings over.

Preparation time: 25 minutes plus chilling

COUNTRY BUMPKIN SOUP

For an even more filling combination, add a large diced potato to the mixture and serve with grated Cheddar cheese.

Serves 4

Ingredients	Metric	Imperial	American
Small cauliflower, cut into small florets	1	1	1
Small swede (rutabaga), cut into small dice	1	1	1
Onion, chopped	1	1	1
Vegetable stock, made with 2 stock cubes	1 litre	1¾ pts	4¼ cups
Salt and pepper			
Tomato purée (paste)	15 ml	1 tbsp	1 tbsp
Dried mixed herbs	5 ml	1 tsp	1 tsp

I. Put all the ingredients in a large saucepan. Bring to the boil, reduce the heat, part-cover and simmer gently for 1 hour until the vegetables are really tender.

2. Taste and re-season if necessary.

Preparation time: 5 minutes
Cooking time: 1 hour

SUMMER CURRIED SWEETCORN

Serves 2

Ingredients	Metric	Imperial	American
Can of sweetcorn (corn), drained	350 g	12 oz	1 large
Dried chives	5 ml	1 tsp	1 tsp
Mayonnaise	15 ml	1 tbsp	1 tbsp
Lemon juice or vinegar	5 ml	1 tsp	1 tsp
Sweet pickle or mango chutney	15 ml	1 tbsp	1 tbsp
Salt and pepper			
Curry powder or paste	10 ml	2 tsp	2 tsp
Shredded lettuce			
Tomato wedges			
To serve: Crusty bread			

1. Mix all the ingredients except the lettuce and tomatoes in a bowl.

2. Pile on a bed of shredded lettuce and arrange a few tomato wedges around.

3. Serve with crusty bread.

 Preparation time: 5 minutes

TOFU- AND TVP-BASED DISHES

FEED ME

Firm tofu makes a great alternative to meat or cheese in recipes. Dried soya mince (TVP) is incredibly cheap and very nutritious, being high in protein and very low in fat. It virtually trebles in weight when reconstituted, so you need only 50 g/2 oz/½ cup dried for a recipe which calls for 175 g/6 oz/1 ½ cups minced (ground) meat or Quorn.

I haven't included any recipes using soya chunks because I don't like them very much. But feel free to experiment with them instead of mince, or throw them in any of the vegetable recipes – they, too, are very cheap.

ORIENTAL TOFU

Make this go round 1 or 2 more people by adding
more peas and a couple of grated carrots to the mixture
and serve with lots of rice!

Serves 2–3

Ingredients	Metric	Imperial	American
Knob of margarine			
Oil	15 ml	1 tbsp	1 tbsp
Packet of firm tofu, cubed	250 g	9 oz	1
Can of broken mandarin orange segments (they're cheaper than whole ones)	312 g	11½ oz	1 small
Frozen peas	50 g	2 oz	½ cup
Ground ginger	2.5 ml	½ tsp	½ tsp
Light brown sugar	15 ml	1 tbsp	1 tbsp
Soy sauce	15 ml	1 tbsp	1 tbsp
Vinegar	15 ml	1 tbsp	1 tbsp
Tomato purée (paste)	15 ml	1 tbsp	1 tbsp
Garlic purée (paste)	2.5 ml	½ tsp	½ tsp
Cornflour (cornstarch)	15 ml	1 tbsp	1 tbsp
Water	15 ml	1 tbsp	1 tbsp
To serve: Boiled rice (see page 15–16)			

I. Heat the margarine and oil in a large frying pan (skillet)
   and fry (sauté) the tofu for about 5 minutes, stirring,
   until golden. Remove from the pan and drain on kitchen
   paper.

2. Drain the mandarin orange segments, reserving the juice in a measuring jug. Make up to 300 ml/½ pt/1¼ cups with water. Stir into the frying pan with the mandarin oranges, peas, tofu and the remaining ingredients except the cornflour and water. Bring to the boil and simmer for 3 minutes.

3. Blend the cornflour with the water and stir into the pan. Cook, stirring, for 2 minutes until thickened. Taste and add more soy sauce if liked.

4. Serve on a bed of boiled rice.

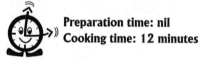

Preparation time: nil
Cooking time: 12 minutes

CHEAPY CHILLI

Serves 2–3

Ingredients	Metric	Imperial	American
Dried soya mince	50 g	2 oz	½ cup
Boiling water			
Oil	10 ml	2 tsp	2 tsp
Small onion, chopped	1	1	1
Tomato purée (paste)	30 ml	2 tbsp	2 tbsp
Garlic purée (paste)	2.5 ml	½ tsp	½ tsp
Chilli powder	2.5 ml	½ tsp	½ tsp
Can of red kidney beans, including the liquid	425 g	15 oz	1 large
Water	150 ml	¼ pt	⅔ cup
Marmite (Vegemite)	15 ml	1 tbsp	1 tbsp
Salt and pepper			

To serve: Shredded lettuce and garlic bread (see page 33)

1. Put the soya mince in a bowl and just cover with boiling water. Stir. Leave to stand until ready to use.

2. Heat the oil in a saucepan and fry (sauté) the onion for 2 minutes, stirring, until softened and lightly golden.

3. Add the soaked mince and the remaining ingredients, stir well. Bring to the boil, reduce the heat to moderate and simmer for 20–30 minutes, stirring occasionally, until the mince and beans are bathed in a rich sauce. If the mixture still looks slightly runny, boil rapidly for a minute or two. Taste and re-season if necessary.

4. Serve in bowls, surrounded by shredded lettuce with garlic bread.

Preparation time: 3 minutes plus standing
Cooking time: 35 minutes

SMOKED TOFU AND BEAN STIR-FRY

To make this go round for a couple more people, simply double the quantity of vegetables and flavourings.

Serves 3

Ingredients	Metric	Imperial	American
Oil	30 ml	2 tbsp	2 tbsp
French (green) beans, topped and tailed and cut into 3 pieces (or use frozen or drained canned beans)	225 g	8 oz	8 oz
Large carrot, cut into matchsticks	1	1	1
Small red (bell) pepper (optional), seeded and cut into strips	1	1	1
Packet of smoked tofu, cubed	225 g	8 oz	1
Light brown sugar	15 ml	1 tbsp	1 tbsp
Vinegar	15 ml	1 tbsp	1 tbsp
Soy sauce	15 ml	1 tbsp	1 tbsp
Chilli powder OR cayenne	1.5 ml	¼ tsp	¼ tsp
Vegetable stock, made with ½ stock cube	150 ml	¼ pt	⅔ cup

To serve: Boiled rice (see page 15–16), noodles or bread

1. **Heat the oil in a wok or large frying pan (skillet). Add the beans, carrot and pepper and stir-fry for 5 minutes. (If using canned beans, add them for the last minute of stir-frying only.)**
2. **Stir in the remaining ingredients, bring to the boil and cook for 7 minutes, stirring occasionally.**
3. **Serve straight away with boiled rice, noodles or bread.**

Preparation time: 5 minutes
Cooking time: 12 minutes

'SMOKEY T' KEDGEREE

This is ideal when you're feeding a few mates. To make it go round for more people, cook a handful of extra rice per person (and up the curry powder a bit), add some more peas and perhaps another hard-boiled egg or 2.

Serves 4

Ingredients	Metric	Imperial	American
Long-grain rice	225 g	8 oz	1 cup
Eggs, scrubbed under the cold tap	2	2	2
Salt			
Knob of margarine			
Onion, chopped	1	1	1
Packet of smoked tofu, cubed	225 g	8 oz	1
Frozen peas	100 g	4 oz	1 cup
Curry powder	5 ml	1 tsp	1 tsp

1. Cook the rice and unshelled eggs in plenty of lightly salted boiling water for 10–15 minutes until the rice is just tender. Drain into a colander. Put the eggs in cold water.

2. Heat the margarine in the saucepan and fry (sauté) the onion for 3 minutes until soft and lightly golden.

3. Add the tofu and peas and fry, stirring, for 4–5 minutes until the peas are tender. Stir in the curry powder, then add the rice and toss well.

4. Shell the eggs and cut in quarters. Add to the pan and toss over a gentle heat until piping hot.

Preparation time: 3 minutes
Cooking time: 25 minutes

VEGETARIAN SPAG BOL

**If you've any dregs of wine lurking, slosh it in.
You'll then need to boil the mixture rapidly at the
end of cooking to reduce the liquid.**

Serves 2

Ingredients	Metric	Imperial	American
Dried soya mince	50 g	2 oz	½ cup
Boiling water			
Oil	10 ml	2 tsp	2 tsp
Onion, chopped	1	1	1
Tomato purée (paste)	15 ml	1 tbsp	1 tbsp
Garlic purée (paste)	5 ml	1 tsp	1 tsp
Can of tomatoes	400 g	14 oz	1 large
Caster (superfine) sugar	5 ml	1 tsp	1 tsp
Dried mixed herbs or basil	2.5 ml	½ tsp	½ tsp

t a pe er

 gh i (co
 pp ite   0 -225   – oz   4   z

 e e: co   e,   ate a sala

P   t s   ce a   v and us c v with o li
w e St   t tar   til r d t u e.

2. **Meanwhile, heat the oil in a saucepan and fry (sauté) the
onion and for 2 minutes, stirring, until it is slightly
softened.**

3. Add the soaked soya mince and the remaining ingredients, except the spaghetti, and break up the tomatoes with a wooden spoon.

4. Bring to the boil, reduce the heat and simmer over a moderate heat for 20–30 minutes, stirring occasionally, until the mixture has formed a rich sauce. Taste and re-season if necessary.

5. Meanwhile, cook the spaghetti in plenty of boiling, lightly salted water (see page 16). Drain and divide between 2 plates.

6. Spoon the sauce over and serve with grated cheese and salad.

Preparation time: 3 minutes plus standing
Cooking time: 35 minutes

LASAGNE AL VORNO

Double the quantities for a great party dish. Providing you use a larger but still shallow dish (even a roasting tin is fine, but brush it with oil first), it won't take any longer to cook.

Serves 3

Ingredients	Metric	Imperial	American
Plain (all-purpose) flour	20 g	¾ oz	3 tbsp
Milk	300 ml	½ pt	1¼ cups
Knob of margarine			
Cheddar cheese, grated	50 g	2 oz	½ cup
Salt and pepper			
1 quantity of vegetarian Spag Bol sauce (see page 66–7)			
No-need-to-precook lasagne sheets	6	6	6

To serve: Salad

Put the flour in a small saucepan and whisk in the milk until smooth. Add the margarine. Bring to the boil, whisking all the time, until thickened and smooth. Cook for 2 minutes still whisking. Stir in the cheese and season to taste.

. Put a thin layer of the Spag Bol sauce in a fairly shallow, ovenproof dish. Top with a layer of lasagne sheets, breaking them to fit. Repeat thin layers of Spag Bol sauce and lasagne, finishing with lasagne. Spoon the cheese sauce over.

3. Bake in a preheated oven at 190°C/375°F/gas mark 5 for about 35 minutes until golden and bubbling, and the lasagne feels tender when a knife is inserted down through the centre.

4. Serve hot with salad.

Preparation time: 40 minutes, including Spag Bol sauce
Cooking time: 40 minutes

COUNTRY COTTAGE PIE

To save time use instant mash.

Serves 3–4

Ingredients	Metric	Imperial	American
Dried soya mince	50 g	2 oz	½ cup
Boiling water			
Oil	10 ml	2 tsp	2 tsp
Onion, chopped	1	1	1
Carrots, finely chopped	3	3	3
Frozen peas	50 g	2 oz	½ cup
Vegetable stock, made with 1 stock cube	300 ml	½ pt	1¼ cups
Marmite (Vegemite)	15 ml	1 tbsp	1 tbsp
Dried mixed herbs	2.5 ml	½ tsp	½ tsp
Plain (all-purpose) flour	30 ml	2 tbsp	2 tbsp

1. Put the soya mince in a bowl and just cover with boiling water. Stir and leave to stand until ready to use.

2. Heat the oil in a flameproof casserole and fry (sauté) the onion for 2 minutes, stirring.

3. Add the soya mince, carrots, peas, stock, Marmite and herbs. Bring to the boil, part-cover, reduce the heat and simmer for 15–20 minutes until the carrots are really tender.

4. Blend the flour with the cold water until smooth. Stir into the pan and cook for 2 minutes until thickened. Taste and season as necessary.

5. Meanwhile, cook the potatoes in boiling, salted water until tender. Drain and mash with the margarine and a little milk. Spoon on top of the soya mixture, then dot with a little more margarine. Place under a hot grill (broiler) until golden brown.

Preparation time: 5 minutes plus standing
Cooking time: 25 minutes

PULSE-BASED DISHES

Dried peas, beans and lentils are a vegetarian's best friend. They're cheap, nutritious and very filling! I've called for cans of them in most recipes because I'm naturally lazy, but if you want to cook your own (which is even cheaper) follow the instructions on page 14 and use about 200 g/4 oz/1 cup dried beans for every 425 g/15 oz/large can.

NOT-SO-MEXICAN TACOS

Serves up to 4 people

Ingredients	Metric	Imperial	American
Taco shells	12	12	12
Oil	30 ml	2 tbsp	2 tbsp
Small onion, chopped	1	1	1
Chilli powder	5 ml	1 tsp	1 tsp
Can of baked beans	400 g	14 oz	1 large
Tomatoes, chopped	2	2	2
Piece of cucumber, chopped	5 cm	2 in	2 in
Salt and pepper			
Cheddar cheese, grated, for topping			

1. **Warm the taco shells according to the packet instructions.**

2. **Heat the oil in a frying pan (skillet) and fry (sauté) the onion for 2 minutes. Add the chilli powder and beans, and mash the beans well with a potato masher. Cook for 2 minutes. Stir in the tomatoes and cucumber and season to taste.**

3. **Spoon into the taco shells, top with some grated cheese and serve straight away.**

Preparation time: 5 minutes
Cooking time: 4 minutes

ROUGH FELAFEL

Serves 2–4

Ingredients	Metric	Imperial	American
Can of chick peas (garbanzos), drained	430 g	15½ oz	1 large
Small onion, very finely chopped	1	1	1
Garlic purée (paste)	5 ml	1 tsp	1 tsp
Chilli powder	2.5 ml	½ tsp	½ tsp
Dried mint (optional)	5 ml	1 tsp	1 tsp
Curry powder or paste	5 ml	1 tsp	1 tsp
Salt and pepper			
Plain (all-purpose) flour	75 g	3 oz	¾ cup
Egg, beaten	1	1	1
Oil for shallow-frying			
Pitta breads	4	4	4
Shredded lettuce			
Slices of cucumber and tomato			

1. Mash the chick peas well with a fork. Stir in the onion, garlic purée, chilli powder, mint and curry powder and season well.

2. Squeeze the mixture well with your hands so it sticks together, then shape into 8 balls. Flatten slightly, then coat with flour. Dip in beaten egg, then flour again.

3. Heat about 5mm/¼ in oil in a frying pan (skillet) and shallow-fry the felafel for about 4 minutes until golden, turning once. Drain on kitchen paper.

4. Split the pitta breads down one edge and open up to form pockets. Put 2 felafel in each pocket and add some lettuce, cucumber and tomato. Eat straight away.

Preparation time: 5 minutes
Cooking time: 4 minutes

TIP: If you don't mash the chick peas well enough, the mixture will be too coarse to stick together. If this happens, add the beaten egg to the mixture, omit the flour, then shallow-fry spoonfuls in hot oil.

QUICK BEAN GRILL

Serves 2

Ingredients	Metric	Imperial	American
Can of ratatouille	425 g	15 oz	1 large
Can of butter beans, drained	200 g	7 oz	1 small
Dried mixed herbs	2.5 ml	½ tsp	½ tsp
Salt and pepper			
Slices of bread, crumbled	2	2	2
Cheddar cheese, grated	50 g	2 oz	½ cup

1. Put the ratatouille, beans and herbs in a small flameproof casserole (Dutch oven) and heat through, stirring. Season to taste if necessary.

2. Mix the crumbs and cheese together and sprinkle over. Place under a hot grill (broiler) until bubbling and t ing en.

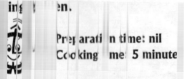

Preparation time: nil
Cooking time 5 minute

LENTIL SUPPER

Serves 2

Ingredients	Metric	Imperial	American
Split red lentils	175 g	6 oz	1 cup
Onion, chopped	1	1	1
Vegetable stock, made with 1 stock cube	450 ml	¾ pt	2 cups
Dried mixed herbs	1.5 ml	¼ tsp	¼ tsp
Salt and pepper			
Weetabix, crumbled	1	1	1
Cheddar cheese, grated	50 g	2 oz	½ cup

To serve: Raw vegetable sticks and tortilla chips OR crispy taco shells

1. Put the lentils, onion and stock in a saucepan. Bring to boil, reduce the heat and simmer for about 15 minutes until the lentils are cooked and have absorbed the liquid.

2. Add the remaining ingredients and heat through for 3 minutes, stirring. Spoon into small bowls.

3. Serve with sticks of raw vegetables either with tortilla chips or spooned into crispy taco shells.

Preparation time: 3 minutes
Cooking time: 18 minutes

MIDWEEK LENTIL MUNCH

If you want to cook this in the evening, put the lentils in a bowl of cold water before you go to college in the morning.

Serves 2–4

Ingredients	Metric	Imperial	American
Brown or green lentils, soaked for at least 2 hours	175 g	6 oz	1 cup
Garlic purée (paste)	2.5 ml	½ tsp	½ tsp
Tomato ketchup (catsup)	15 ml	1 tbsp	1 tbsp
Sweet pickle or brown table sauce	10 ml	2 tsp	2 tsp
Soy sauce	5 ml	1 tsp	1 tsp
Salt and pepper			
Cheddar cheese, grated	175 g	6 oz	1½ cups
To serve: Green salad			

1. Dai te al nd place n sma f or c sc ou Coer wi ar, ri o t bl, e us th t-over nd simer b 4 rmte u

2. D ai ad et aserole St i te in in rlit a t tee-aes t e Srid t r eee on o e ba n preheated oven at 200°C/400°F/gas mark 6 for about 20 minutes until turning golden on top.

3. Serve with a green salad.

Preparation time: 2 minutes plus soaking
Cooking time: 1 hour 5 minutes

MIXED PULSE SCRAMBLE

Serves 2

Ingredients	Metric	Imperial	American
Can of mixed pulses, drained	430 g	15½ oz	1 large
Knob of margarine			
Egg, beaten	1	1	1
Cheddar cheese, grated	50 g	2 oz	½ cup
Salt and pepper			
Pinch of chilli powder			
Milk	30 ml	2 tbsp	2 tbsp
To serve: Toast and sliced tomatoes			

I. Put all the ingredients in a saucepan and cook gently, stirring all the time, until scrambled. Do not allow to boil.

2. Pile on to hot toast and serve straight away with sliced tomatoes.

Preparation time: nil
Cooking time: 5 minutes

BAKED BEAN LOAF

**This is great cold the next day with
French bread and pickles.**

Serves 4

Ingredients	Metric	Imperial	American
Can of baked beans	400 g	14 oz	1 large
Small onion, chopped	1	1	1
Slices of bread, crumbled	2	2	2
Tomato ketchup (catsup)	30 ml	2 tbsp	2 tbsp
Egg, beaten	1	1	1
Marmite (Vegemite)	5 ml	1 tsp	1 tsp
Dried mixed herbs	5 ml	1 tsp	1 tsp
Salt and pepper			

To serve: Potatoes, carrots and vegetarian gravy (see page 90)

P   a t l gr   s i a   l   t mi   w ll.

T n   nt a re   50 g   lc   t , r er ol li d
w h re e ,   rc f   e   p pe   r a gr as d,
o n ro f is   in   ea l ve   1 0 C/
3 0° /g   a   a   n es o un l e
n t re el s   e o

3. C ol lig tl , t   dg   it a o d bl le
knife and turn out of the tin.

4. Serve cut into slices (or serve straight from the dish) with
potatoes, carrots and vegetarian gravy.

**Preparation time: 5 minutes
Cooking time: 30 minutes**

MIXED BEAN SALAD

Serves 4

Ingredients	Metric	Imperial	American
Small onion, chopped	1	1	1
Garlic purée (paste)	2.5 ml	½ tsp	½ tsp
Oil	45 ml	3 tbsp	3 tbsp
Vinegar	15 ml	1 tbsp	1 tbsp
Salt and pepper			
Can of red kidney beans, drained	425 g	15 oz	1 large
Can of butter beans, drained	425 g	15 oz	1 large
Can of broad (lima) beans, drained	300 g	11 oz	1 small
Can of cut French beans, drained	300 g	11 oz	1 small
Lettuce leaves			
Hard-boiled (hard-cooked) eggs (see page 12), roughly chopped	2	2	2
To serve: Crusty bread			

1. Whisk the onion, garlic purée, oil, vinegar and a little salt and pepper in a bowl.

2. Add the drained beans and toss gently but well.

3. Pile on to lettuce leaves on 4 plates and top with the chopped egg. Serve with crusty bread.

Preparation time: 5 minutes
Cooking time: nil

GREEK-STYLE CHICK PEA SALAD

This is good hot with rice, too.

Serves 2

Ingredients	Metric	Imperial	American
Onion, chopped	1	1	1
Oil	30 ml	2 tbsp	2 tbsp
Can of tomatoes	400 g	14 oz	1 large
Tomato purée (paste)	15 ml	1 tbsp	1 tbsp
Garlic purée (paste)	5 ml	1 tsp	1 tsp
Dried mixed herbs	2.5 ml	½ tsp	½ tsp
Vinegar	15 ml	1 tbsp	1 tbsp
Can of chick peas (garbanzos), drained	430 g	15½ oz	1 large
Salt and pepper			

Preparation time: 2 minutes
Cooking time: 5 minutes plus cooling
and chilling

'ROAST' DISHES

FEED ME

Non-vegetarians often have a strange concept of nut roasts and cutlet-type dishes. They think they're 'cranky'. They're not, they're absolutely delicious and a great way of filling up lots of people with lots of goodness. If you like your food moist, there are a couple of recipes for vegetarian gravy in this section or you could always heat a can of tomatoes, well mashed, to form a chunky sauce. Alternatively, you could go mad and buy a jar of passata (sieved tomatoes) for a smooth alternative. But remember to keep it in the fridge once opened or it'll go off. A final choice would be to heat a can of condensed mushroom, tomato or celery soup, thin with milk to the consistency you like and serve that with the roast.

BASIC NUT ROAST

Prepare your vegetables for roasting and put in the oven on the top shelf before you prepare the nut roast. Then they'll all be ready about the same time.

Serves 4

Ingredients	Metric	Imperial	American
Marmite (Vegemite)	10 ml	2 tsp	2 tsp
Boiling water	150 ml	¼ pt	⅔ cup
Chopped mixed nuts	150 g	5 oz	1¼ cups
Slices of wholemeal bread, crumbled	3	3	3
Small onion, finely chopped	1	1	1
Soy sauce	20 ml	4 tsp	4 tsp
Dried mixed herbs	2.5 ml	½ tsp	½ tsp
Melted margarine	30 ml	2 tbsp	2 tbsp
	5 ml	1 tsp	1 tsp

and press down gently.

4. Roast in a preheated oven at 190°C/375°F/gas mark 5 for 30–40 minutes until crisp on top and hot through.

5. Serve with roast vegetables and mushroom gravy.

Preparation time: 5 minutes
Cooking time: 40 minutes

POOR STUDENT'S ROAST

Vegetable suet is available in the baking section of any good supermarket.

Serves 4

Ingredients	Metric	Imperial	American
Marmite (Vegemite)	10 ml	2 tsp	2 tsp
Milk	30 ml	2 tbsp	2 tbsp
Plain (all-purpose) flour	100 g	4 oz	1 cup
Porridge oats	100 g	4 oz	1 cup
Slices of wholemeal bread, crumbled	2	2	2
Shredded vegetable suet	175 g	6 oz	1½ cups
Large onions, chopped	2	2	2
Dried mixed herbs	5 ml	1 tsp	1 tsp
Egg, beaten	1	1	1
Salt and pepper			

To serve: Roast potatoes and carrots (see page 15) and vegetarian gravy

1. Blend the Marmite with the milk in a large bowl.

2. Stir in the remaining ingredients and season well with salt and pepper. Add a little more milk if necessary to form a soft but not sloppy mixture.

3. Turn into a greased roasting tin (pan) and level the surface.

4. Roast in a preheated oven at 180°C/350°F/gas mark 4 for about 1 hour or until it is golden brown and the mixture feels set when pressed.

5. Serve hot with roast potatoes and carrots and gravy.

Preparation time: 5 minutes
Cooking time: 1 hour

SAGE AND ONION ROAST

Serves 4

Ingredients	Metric	Imperial	American
Oil	30 ml	2 tbsp	2 tbsp
Onions, chopped	2	2	2
Cans of any dried beans or lentils, drained	2 × 425 g	2 × 15 oz	2 large
Chopped mixed nuts	100 g	4 oz	1 cup
Edam cheese, grated	100 g	4 oz	1 cup
Dried sage	5 ml	1 tsp	1 tsp
Marmite (Vegemite)	5 ml	1 tsp	1 tsp
Eggs, beaten	2	2	2
Salt and pepper			

To serve: Roast potatoes, a green vegetable and vegetarian gravy (see page 90)

Heat the oil in a large saucepan and dry (sauté) the onions for a minutes, stirring

Add the drained beans or lentils and mash thoroughly with a fork or potato masher

Stir in the remaining ingredients and mix together

4. **Turn into a greased 450 g/1 lb loaf tin or any ovenproof dish and press down lightly.**

5. Roast in a preheated oven at 190°C/375°F/gas mark 5 for about 30–40 minutes or until the mixture feels set when lightly pressed. Leave to cool slightly, then turn out if in a tin.

6. Serve with roast potatoes, a green vegetable and vegetarian gravy.

Preparation time: 10 minutes
Cooking time: 40 minutes

VEGGIE BURGERS

**Shape the same mixture into 4–6 sausages
and serve in finger rolls with fried onions,
ketchup (catsup) and mustard.**

Serves 4

Ingredients	Metric	Imperial	American
Porridge oats	100 g	4 oz	1 cup
Wholemeal flour	75 g	3 oz	¾ cup
Carrots, grated	4	4	4
Cheddar cheese, grated	50 g	2 oz	½ cup
Small onion, finely chopped	1	1	1
Tomato purée (paste)	15 ml	1 tbsp	1 tbsp
Soy sauce	15 ml	1 tbsp	1 tbsp
Dried mixed herbs	5 ml	1 tsp	1 tsp
Salt and pepper			
Egg, beaten	1	1	1
Oil for shallow frying			
To serve: Burger buns, salad and dill pickle slices			

1. Mix all the ingredients together, keeping the oats, shape into fairly large burgers.

2. Heat about 5 mm/¼ in oil in a large frying pan, non-stick and fry (sauté) the burgers for 5 minutes, turning once until cooked through and golden brown.

3. Serve in burger buns with salad and dill pickle slices.

**Preparation time: 5 minutes
Cooking time: 5 minutes**

NUTTY BEAN BURGERS

Serves 4

Ingredients	Metric	Imperial	American
Can of aduki beans, drained	425 g	15 oz	1 large
Carrot, grated	1	1	1
Small parsnip, grated	1	1	1
Chopped mixed nuts	25 g	1 oz	¼ cup
Slices of bread, crumbled	2	2	2
Marmite (Vegemite)	5 ml	1 tsp	1 tsp
Salt and pepper			
Egg, beaten	1	1	1
Oil for shallow-frying			
To serve: Chips and salad			

1. **Mash the beans well in a bowl. Add the remaining ingredients except the oil, using enough of the beaten egg to bind the mixture together without making it too wet.**

2. **Shape into 4 burgers and chill, if there is time, for 30 minutes. Heat about 5 mm/¼ in hot oil in a frying pan (skillet) and shallow-fry until golden brown on both sides. Drain on kitchen paper.**

3. **Serve with chips and salad.**

Preparation time: 5 minutes plus chilling
Cooking time: 10 minutes

VEGETARIAN GRAVY

Makes about 300 ml/½ pt/1¼ cups

Ingredients	Metric	Imperial	American
Margarine	50 g	2 oz	¼ cup
Onions, finely chopped	2	2	2
Plain (all-purpose) flour	15 g	½ oz	2 tbsp
Vegetable stock, made with 1 stock cube	300 ml	½ pt	1¼ cups
Worcestershire sauce	5 ml	1 tsp	1 tsp
Marmite (Vegemite)	5 ml	1 tsp	1 tsp
Salt and pepper			

1. Melt the margarine and fry (sauté) the onions for 5 minutes, stirring, until golden brown.

2. Stir in the flour, then blend in the stock and the

MUSHROOM GRAVY

Makes about 450 ml/¾ pt/2 cups

Prepare as for Vegetarian Gravy (above) but add 50 g/2 oz/1 cup sliced or chopped mushrooms for the last 2 minutes when cooking the onions. Then continue as above but don't strain the gravy at the end.

RICE-BASED DISHES

Rice comes in many shapes and forms. I've used ordinary long-grain for most of these recipes as it's the most economical, plus some brown rice as it's so good for you. Obviously basmati and other more exotic sorts of rice have a terrific flavour and are worth using if you want to impress but you'll have to pay the price! The recipes nearly all serve four people as most of them are good eaten cold the next day.

BAKED VEGETABLE RISOTTO

Serves 4

Ingredients	Metric	Imperial	American
Oil	45 ml	3 tbsp	3 tbsp
Onion, chopped	1	1	1
Long-grain rice	150 g	5 oz	⅔ cup
Curry powder	10 ml	2 tsp	2 tsp
Chilli powder (optional)	5 ml	1 tsp	1 tsp
Carrot, chopped	1	1	1
Green or red (bell) pepper, seeds removed and chopped	1	1	1
Frozen peas	50 g	2 oz	½ cup
Can of sweetcorn (corn)	200 g	7 oz	1 small
Garlic purée (paste)	5 ml	1 tsp	1 tsp
Vegetable stock		¼ pt	2
Pine nuts		oz	½
Salt and pepper			

1. Heat the oil in a flameproof (Dutch) oven.

2. Add the onion and fry (sauté) for 5 minutes, stirring.

3. Add the rice and stir until coated with the oil, then add
   the remaining ingredients. Stir well and bring to the boil.

4. Cover and place in a preheated oven at 180°C/350°F/ gas mark 4 for 30–40 minutes until the rice and vegetables are tender and all the liquid has been absorbed. Stir well before serving.

 Preparation time: 5 minutes
Cooking time: 40 minutes

SPECIAL TOMATO RICE SOUP

Serves 4

Ingredients	Metric	Imperial	American
Handful of long-grain rice			
Can of tomatoes	400 g	14 oz	1 large
Can of cream of tomato soup	295 g	10½ oz	1 small
Worcestershire sauce			

1. Put the rice in a saucepan with the tomatoes and break them up with a wooden spoon.

2. Half-fill the tomato can with water and add to the pan. Bring to the boil, reduce the heat and simmer for 10 minutes until the rice is just tender, stirring occasionally.

3. Stir in the can of tomato soup and spike to taste with Worcestershire sauce. Heat through and serve.

 Preparation time: nil
Cooking time: 15 minutes

LEFTOVER STUFFED PEPPERS

Serves 4

Ingredients	Metric	Imperial	American
Red or green (bell) peppers	4	4	4
Eggs, beaten	2	2	2
Cold cooked Baked Vegetable Risotto (see page 92)	225 g	8 oz	2 cups
To serve: Salad and crusty bread			

1. Cut a slice off the stalk end of the peppers and remove the seeds. Level the bases so they stand upright, taking care not to make holes in the peppers.

2. Mix the beaten eggs and risotto together and pack into the peppers. Lay the stalk ends on top.

3. ...in the tu...s ba...ng (...an) a...d ...rt ...ll ti...in ...ter

4. ...ke...n...re...n ...0°/40...°F ...as m...ark 6 or ...u...ppre...end...and the fill...g is ...i...

5. ...r...s...gh...n s...al...an...cr...ty...read

Preparation time: 10 minutes
Cooking time: 30 minutes

CREAMY CHEESE AND SPINACH RICE

Serves 4

Ingredients	Metric	Imperial	American
Knob of margarine			
Oil	30 ml	2 tbsp	2 tbsp
Small onion, chopped	1	1	1
Long-grain rice	150 g	5 oz	⅔ cup
Vegetable stock, made with 1 or 2 stock cubes	600 ml	1 pt	2½ cups
Dried mixed herbs	5 ml	1 tsp	1 tsp
Salt and pepper			
Frozen chopped spinach	175 g	6 oz	6 oz
Single (light) cream or evaporated milk	45 ml	3 tbsp	3 tbsp
Pecorino cheese, grated	50 g	2 oz	½ cup

1. Melt the margarine with the oil in a saucepan. Add the onion and fry (sauté) for 2 minutes, stirring.
2. Add the rice and stir until coated in the oil and margarine.
3. Add the stock, herbs and a little salt and pepper, and simmer for 15–20 minutes, stirring occasionally.
4. Add the spinach and cook for a further 5 minutes. Stir in the cream or milk. The rice should be soft and creamy, not dry and separate.
5. Lastly stir in the cheese and re-season if necessary.
6. Serve hot straight from the pan.

Preparation time: 3 minutes
Cooking time: about 30 minutes

CASHEW PAELLA

Cashew nuts are a bit extravagant but they taste fantastic.
For a more economical dish, substitute peanuts.

Serves 4

Ingredients	Metric	Imperial	American
Oil	15 ml	1 tbsp	1 tbsp
Leek, chopped	1	1	1
Red (bell) pepper, seeds removed and chopped	1	1	1
Green (bell) pepper, seeds removed and chopped	1	1	1
Mushrooms, sliced	100 g	4 oz	4 oz
Long-grain rice	225 g	8 oz	1 cup
Unroasted cashew nuts	100 g	4 oz	1 cup
Vegetable stock, made with 2 stock cubes	600 ml	1 pt	2½ cups
ri d n ix d l r	2.5	t	½
erve: S al			

1. He at th o i a e p n fi (s u) o e bl ov er e e ea r 5 n t es ti i g.

2. A d t h r e d u il c te in i

3. Add the remaining ingredients, bring to the boil, reduce
   the heat, cover and simmer gently for about 20 minutes
   until the rice is cooked and has absorbed the liquid. Stir
   gently once or twice.

4. Serve hot with salad.

Preparation time: 5 minutes
Cooking time: 25 minutes

TIP: Don't be fooled into thinking it's cheaper to buy 3 peppers already pre-packed; they are much cheaper bought separately!

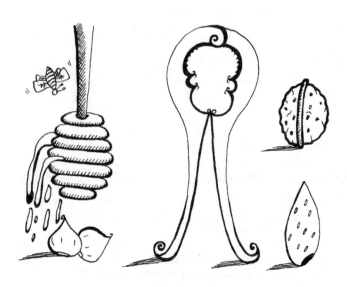

RICE AND LENTIL CASSEROLE

Serves 4

Ingredients	Metric	Imperial	American
Green lentils, rinsed	100 g	4 oz	⅔ cup
Long-grain rice	175 g	6 oz	¾ cup
Knob of margarine			
Oil	15 ml	1 tbsp	1 tbsp
Onion, chopped	1	1	1
Carrots, finely chopped	2	2	2
Tomato purée (paste)	15 ml	1 tbsp	1 tbsp
Water	15 ml	1 tbsp	1 tbsp
Curry powder	5 ml	1 tsp	1 tsp
Salt and pepper			

the rice and lentils and the curry powder. Season with
salt and pepper. Cook for 3 minutes, stirring.

4. Serve spooned into pitta bread pockets.

Preparation time: 5 minutes
Cooking time: 35 minutes

SPICY FRIED RICE AND BEANS

Serves 2

Ingredients	Metric	Imperial	American
Knob of margarine			
Onion, finely chopped	1	1	1
Curry powder	10 ml	2 tsp	2 tsp
Chilli powder	1.5 ml	¼ tsp	¼ tsp
Cooked long-grain rice (about 75 g/3 oz/⅓ cup uncooked weight)	175 g	6 oz	1½ cups
Can of black-eyed beans, drained	425 g	15 oz	1 large

To serve: Cucumber raita (chopped cucumber, mixed into yoghurt and flavoured with dried mint and a dash of garlic purée), mango or other chutney and naan bread

1. **Melt the margarine in a saucepan, add the onion and spices and fry (sauté) for 3 minutes.**

2. **Add the rice and beans and stir-fry for 4–5 minutes until piping hot.**

3. **Serve hot with cucumber raita, chutney and naan bread.**

Preparation time: 5 minutes
Cooking time: 10 minutes

ORIENTAL PILAF

I've called for ground ginger, but fresh root ginger is much
better in this and most other Chinese-style recipes.
If you're feeling flush, you can buy it ready-puréed
in a small jar or buy a piece of knobbly root which
you peel and grate or chop finely.

Serves 4

Ingredients	Metric	Imperial	American
Knob of margarine			
Bunch of spring onions (scallions), chopped	1	1	1
Long-grain rice	225 g	8 oz	1 cup
Ground ginger	5 ml	1 tsp	1 tsp
Soy sauce	10 ml	2 tsp	2 tsp
Chilli powder	2.5 ml	½ tsp	½ tsp
Vegetable stock, made with ck be	600 ml	1 pt	2½ cups
ck f f tofu, cu d	250 g	oz	1
ai i	50	oz	⅓ cup
o e: tra soy s ce d sa un s or ni r fruit se; mente			

1. Melt the margarine in a saucepan. Add the onions and
(sauté) for a minute stirring

2. Add the rice and stir to coat with margarine.

3. Add the remaining ingredients except the tofu and
raisins and simmer for 10 minutes. Add the tofu and
raisins and continue cooking for a further 10 minutes
until the rice is tender and has absorbed the liquid.

4. Spoon on to warm plates and sprinkle a little extra soy sauce over. Arrange segments of satsuma around and serve.

Preparation time: 2 minutes
Cooking time: 25 minutes

VEGGIE RICE WITH EGG SUPPER

Serves 2

Ingredients	Metric	Imperial	American
Long-grain rice	100 g	4 oz	½ cup
Vegetable stock cube	1	1	1
Frozen mixed vegetables	75 g	3 oz	¾ cup
Worcestershire sauce to taste			
Eggs	4	4	4

1. Cook the rice for 10 minutes in plenty of boiling water to which the stock cube has been added. Add the vegetables and cook for a further 6–8 minutes until the rice and vegetables are tender. Drain.

2. Meanwhile, poach the eggs (see page 12), or fry if you prefe

3. S o   he ic on t wa m plates T o wit   the eggs an
   a d   o sl sh of Wo cestershi e auce.

   P para on me: nil
   → C okin tim : about 2 n utes

CUBAN RICE AND EGGS

This is one of the exceptions to the eating cold the next day rule – eat and enjoy as soon as you've cooked it.

Serves 2

Ingredients	Metric	Imperial	American
Long-grain rice	100 g	4 oz	½ cup
Small onion, chopped	1	1	1
Garlic purée (paste)	2.5 ml	½ tsp	½ tsp
Oil	45 ml	3 tbsp	3 tbsp
Banana, cut into chunks	1	1	1
Eggs	2	2	2
Salt and pepper			
To serve: Salad			

1. Cook the rice in plenty of boiling, salted water for 10–15 minutes or until just tender. Drain in a colander and keep warm over the saucepan with a little simmering water in it.
2. Meanwhile, fry (sauté) the onion and garlic in a third of the oil in a frying pan (skillet) until golden brown. Remove from the pan with a fish slice and add to the rice.
3. Add a further 15 ml/1 tbsp of the oil to the frying pan and fry the banana, stirring, for about 2 minutes until just cooked but still holding its shape. Add to the rice.
4. Heat the remaining oil and fry the eggs. Mix the rice gently with the onions and banana, season well.
5. Pile on to warm plates. Top each pile with an egg and serve with salad.

Preparation time: 2 minutes
Cooking time: 10–15 minutes

BROWN RICE MOUNTAIN

Serves 4

Ingredients	Metric	Imperial	American
Margarine	50 g	2 oz	¼ cup
Onion, finely chopped	1	1	1
Broccoli, cut into small florets	225 g	8 oz	8 oz
Small cauliflower, cut into small florets	1	1	1
Carrots, sliced	2	2	2
Brown rice	175 g	6 oz	¾ cup
Can of chick peas (garbanzos)	430 g	15½ oz	1 large
Vegetable stock, made with 2 stock cubes	750 ml	1¼ pts	3 cups
Marmite (Vegemite)	10 ml	2 tsp	2 tsp
Dried mixed herbs	5 ml	1 tsp	1 tsp
alt and pepper			
o serve: Pecori ch a			

In a large m   c sero   (Dutch oven),   elt th
m argarine   nd   u   ) the prepared vegetal es fo
4 minutes, tir

. Add the ri   a   f   1 m   ute.

3. Add the chick peas. Blend the stock and Marmite
together, pour over and bring to the boil. Add the herbs,
cover and bake in a preheated oven at 200°C/400°F/gas
mark 6 for about 40 minutes until the vegetables and
rice are tender and the rice has absorbed the liquid. Stir
well, taste and re-season if necessary. Serve sprinkled
with grated Pecorino cheese.

Preparation time: 5 minutes
Cooking time: 45 minutes

EGG TOP

Prepare as for Brown Rice Mountain but after 25 minutes'
cooking, beat 3 eggs with 2.5 ml/½ tsp garlic purée and a
little salt and pepper and pour over the top of the rice. Cover
and continue cooking for a further 10 minutes or until the
eggs are set and the rice is cooked.
Serve straight from the pan. Serves 4–6.

BROWN RICE AND CHEESE SALAD

To make this even more substantial, add a handful
of nuts or mixed nuts and raisins.

Serves 4

Ingredients	Metric	Imperial	American
Brown rice	175 g	6 oz	¾ cup
Frozen mixed vegetables	100 g	4 oz	1 cup
Oil	30 ml	2 tbsp	2 tbsp
Vinegar	15 ml	1 tbsp	1 tbsp
Salt and pepper			
Cheddar cheese, cubed	175 g	6 oz	1½ cups
Eating (dessert) apple, cored and diced	1	1	1
Mayonnaise	30 ml	2 tbsp	2 tbsp

1. Cook the rice in plenty of boiling, salted water for about 35–40 minutes or until tender. Add the vegetables after 3 minutes. Drain in a colander, rinse with cold water and drain again.

2. Mix the oil, vinegar and a little salt and pepper and pile into nests on 4 serving plates.

3. Mix the cheese and apple with the mayonnaise and a little salt and pepper and spoon in to the centres.

Preparation time: 5 minutes
Cooking time: 40 minutes

INDIAN-STYLE RICE SALAD

**If you're not planning to eat all this at one meal,
do not add the banana to the portion you're setting aside
as it won't keep too well overnight.**

Serves 4

Ingredients	Metric	Imperial	American
Long-grain rice	175 g	6 oz	¾ cup
Curry powder	15 ml	1 tbsp	1 tbsp
Mayonnaise	45 ml	3 tbsp	3 tbsp
Raisins	50 g	2 oz	⅓ cup
Creamed coconut, grated OR desiccated (shredded) coconut	50 g	2 oz	½ cup
Can of sweetcorn (corn), drained	200 g	7 oz	1 small
Piece of cucumber, diced	5 cm	2 in	2 in
Banana, sliced and tossed in a little lemon juice or vinegar to prevent browning	1	1	1

To serve: Popadoms

1. Cook the rice in plenty of boiling, salted water for 10–15 minutes or until tender. Drain in a colander, rinse with cold water and drain again.
2. Mix the curry powder and mayonnaise in a bowl.
3. Add the rice and the remaining ingredients and toss gently but thoroughly.
4. Serve with popadoms.

**Preparation time: 5 minutes
Cooking time: 10–15 minutes**

PASTA-BASED DISHES

Pasta is a great filler – cheap, versatile and good for you, too.

At its simplest, cooked until just tender, then tossed with a little

marga... ... ...e grated cheese, it's fine ...ee he...

...ag 1... ...ry ...ci ...g. ...lere a...e ...m in...ov...

...i ex...p... ...lea... as ...wa...s wit... It...y ...be...t...

NOODLE SOUP

To turn this into a more filling main meal, add
a poached egg (see page 12) to each soup bowl
before pouring on the hot soup.

Serves 4

Ingredients	Metric	Imperial	American
Vegetable stock, made with 3 stock cubes	1.75 litres	3 pts	7½ cups
Vermicelli	225 g	8 oz	8 oz
Pinch of ground ginger (optional)			
Soy sauce			

I. Bring the stock to the boil in a saucepan.

2. Crumble in the vermicelli so it is broken into small pieces.

3. Add the ginger, if using, and soy sauce to taste. Bring back to the boil. Simmer uncovered for 5 minutes until the noodles are cooked. Taste and add more soy sauce if liked.

Preparation time: nil
Cooking time: 15 minutes

SPAGHETTI WITH LENTILS AND TOMATOES

If you haven't got 4 people to feed, eat some today and use the rest spooned over boiled rice for another meal.

Serves 4

Ingredients	Metric	Imperial	American
Green lentils	100 g	4 oz	⅔ cup
Can of tomatoes	400 g	14 oz	1 large
Vegetable stock, made with 1 stock cube	600 ml	1 pt	2½ cups
Onion, chopped	1	1	1
Dried basil	5 ml	1 tsp	1 tsp
Salt and pepper			
Spaghetti (or according to appetites)	225 g	8 oz	8 oz
Pecorino cheese, grated			

3. Meanwhile, cook the spaghetti (see page 16) and drain. Pile on to plates and spoon the sauce over. Sprinkle with grated Pecorino cheese and serve.

Preparation time: 5 minutes
Cooking time: 30 minutes

LAZY LASAGNE

Serves 3–4

Ingredients	Metric	Imperial	American
Can of ratatouille	425 g	15 oz	1 large
Can of sweetcorn (corn)	200 g	7 oz	1 small
Dried mixed herbs	2.5 ml	½ tsp	½ tsp
No-need-to-precook lasagne	6 sheets	6 sheets	6 sheets
Plain (all-purpose) flour	45 ml	3 tbsp	3 tbsp
Milk	300 ml	½ pt	1 ¼ cups
Knob of margarine			
Salt and pepper			
Cheddar cheese, grated	100 g	4 oz	1 cup
To serve: Salad			

1. Mix the ratatouille, sweetcorn and herbs together.
2. Layer the mixture and the lasagne sheets in a shallow ovenproof dish, ending with a layer of lasagne.
3. Whisk the flour with the milk in a saucepan. Add the margarine, bring to the boil and cook for 2 minutes, whisking all the time. Stir in half the cheese and season to taste.
4. Spoon the sauce over the lasagne and sprinkle with the remaining cheese. Bake in a preheated oven at 190°C/375°F/gas mark 5 for 35 minutes or until bubbling and golden brown. The lasagne should feel tender when a knife is inserted down through the centre.
5. Serve with salad.

Preparation time: 10 minutes
Cooking time: 35 minutes

QUICK PASTA BAKE

Serves 4

Ingredients	Metric	Imperial	American
Pasta shapes	225 g	8 oz	8 oz
Eggs, scrubbed under the cold tap	2–3	2–3	2–3
Can of tomatoes	400 g	14 oz	1 large
Dried basil or mixed herbs	5 ml	1 tsp	1 tsp
Frozen spinach, thawed	175 g	6 oz	6 oz
Milk	300 ml	½ pt	1¼ cups
Plain (all-purpose) flour	45 ml	3 tbsp	3 tbsp
Knob of margarine			
Cheddar cheese, grated	75 g	3 oz	¾ cup
Salt and pepper			

1. Cook the pasta and eggs (shelled) in plenty of boiling water for 10 minutes or until the pasta is just tender. Drain in a colander and plunge the eggs in cold water. Put a layer of half the pasta in an ovenproof dish.

2. Chop up the tomatoes and spoon half over the pasta. Sprinkle with half of the basil or herbs and spread all the spinach over.

3. Shell the eggs and cut in slices. Lay over the spinach. Top with the remaining pasta then the remaining tomatoes and sprinkle with the remaining herbs.

4. Whisk the milk and flour in the pasta saucepan until smooth. Add the margarine and bring to the boil, whisking all the time. Cook for 2 minutes, stirring, until thickened. Add half the cheese and season to taste.

5. Pour over the pasta and top with the remaining cheese.
   Cook in a preheated oven at 200°C/400°F/gas mark 6
   for about 30 minutes or until golden brown and piping
   hot.

Preparation time: 10 minutes
Cooking time: 45 minutes

WALNUT AND MUSHROOM TAGLIATELLE

Walnut pieces are cheaper than halves because they're the broken ones.

Serves 2–4

Ingredients	Metric	Imperial	American
Tagliatelle (or according to appetites)	225 g	8 oz	8 oz
Knob of margarine			
Onion, thinly sliced	1	1	1
Mushrooms, sliced	225 g	8 oz	8 oz
Walnut pieces, roughly chopped	75 g	3 oz	¾ cup
Single (light) cream	150 ml	¼ pt	⅔ cup
Plain yoghurt	150 ml	¼ pt	⅔ cup
Dried mixed herbs	2.5 ml	½ tsp	½ tsp
Salt and pepper			
To serve: Tomato salad			

1. Cook the tagliatelle according to the packet directions. Drain in a colander.

2. Melt the margarine in the same pan and fry (sauté) the onion for 4 minutes until soft and turning golden.

3. Add the remaining ingredients and heat through, stirring. Add the tagliatelle, toss well.

4. Serve hot with a tomato salad.

Preparation time: 5 minutes
Cooking time: 15 minutes

TORTELLINI WITH TOMATO SAUCE

Serves 2

Ingredients	Metric	Imperial	American
Dried tortellini with either cheese, spinach and ricotta or mushroom filling	250 g	9 oz	9 oz
Can of tomatoes, chopped	400 g	14 oz	1 large
Tomato purée (paste)	15 ml	1 tbsp	1 tbsp
Garlic purée (paste)	2.5 ml	½ tsp	½ tsp
Dried basil	2.5 ml	½ tsp	½ tsp
Salt and pepper			

To serve: Pecorino cheese, grated, and a green salad

1. Cook the stuffed pasta according to packet directions. Drain and return to the saucepan.

2. Drain the liquid from the tomatoes into the saucepan and snip the tomatoes with scissors so they are cut small. Add to the pan with the herbs and a little salt and pepper.

3. Heat through, stirring, then spoon on to plates.

4. Sprinkle with Pecorino cheese and serve with a green salad.

Preparation time: 5 minutes
Cooking time: 20 minutes

RIGATONI RIGALETTO

Serves 4

Ingredients	Metric	Imperial	American
Margarine	50 g	2 oz	¼ cup
Bunch of spring onions (scallions), chopped			
Mushrooms, sliced	350 g	12 oz	12 oz
Frozen peas	100 g	4 oz	1 cup
Single (light) cream	150 ml	¼ pt	⅔ cup
Plain yoghurt	150 ml	¼ pt	⅔ cup
Salt and pepper			
Rigatoni	225 g	8 oz	8 oz

To serve: Crusty bread and a green salad

I. Melt the margarine in a saucepan, add the spring onions, mushrooms and peas and cook, stirring, for 2 minutes. Reduce the heat, cover and simmer gently for 10 minutes, stirring occasionally. Stir in the cream and yoghurt and season to taste.

Meanwhile, cook the rigatoni according to the packet directions. Drain, add to the sauce and toss well.

Serve straight away with crusty bread and a green salad.

Preparation time: 5 minutes
Cooking time: 15 minutes

SPEEDY PASTA GRILL

Serves 4

Ingredients	Metric	Imperial	American
Pasta shapes	225 g	8 oz	8 oz
Can of tomatoes	400 g	14 oz	1 large
Can of red kidney beans, drained	425 g	15 oz	1 large
Garlic purée (paste)	5 ml	1 tsp	1 tsp
Dried basil	5 ml	1 tsp	1 tsp
Cheddar cheese, grated	50 g	2 oz	½ cup
Slices of bread, crumbled	2	2	2

To serve: Shredded white cabbage tossed in a little oil, vinegar and some salt and pepper.

1. **Cook the pasta according to the packet directions but in a flameproof casserole (Dutch oven) rather than an ordinary saucepan. Drain, and return to the casserole.**

2. **Add the can of tomatoes and break up well with a wooden spoon.**

3. **Add the beans, garlic purée, basil and some salt and pepper and heat through until piping hot.**

4. **Mix the cheese and breadcrumbs together and scatter over the top. Place under a hot grill (broiler) until golden and the cheese has melted.**

5. **Serve with a shredded cabbage salad.**

 Preparation time: 5 minutes
Cooking time: 20 minutes

MACARONI CHEESE

Serves 2–4

Ingredients	Metric	Imperial	American
Quick-cook macaroni	175 g	6 oz	6 oz
Plain (all-purpose) flour	20 g	¾ oz	3 tbsp
Milk	300 ml	½ pt	1¼ cups
Knob of margarine			
Dried mixed herbs	2.5 ml	½ tsp	½ tsp
Mustard (optional)	5 ml	1 tsp	1 tsp
Salt and pepper			
Cheddar cheese, grated	100 g	4 oz	1 cup
To serve: Can of tomatoes			

1. **Cook the macaroni according to the packet directions. Drain in a colander.**

2. **Whisk the flour and milk together in a saucepan until smooth. Add the margarine. Bring to the boil and cook for 2 minutes, whisking all the time until smooth and thickened.**

3. **Stir in the herbs, mustard, if using, seasoning to taste and the cheese. Add the macaroni. Stir over a gentle heat until piping hot, then spoon on to plates and serve with tomatoes. Alternatively, add three-quarters of the cheese to the sauce, add the macaroni, heat through and spoon into a flameproof dish. Top with the remaining cheese and grill (broil) until golden and bubbling before serving with the canned tomatoes.**

Preparation time: 5 minutes
Cooking time: 20 minutes

ANYTHING GOES PASTA SALAD

There are no quantities or servings for this, but as a guide allow 50 g/2 oz pasta shapes per person and cook according to the packet directions. Drain, rinse with cold water and drain again. Then add whatever combination of ingredients you have available. For instance, grated carrot, chopped tomato and/or cucumber, nuts, raisins, chopped apple or other fruit, drained, canned vegetables or pulses, sliced mushrooms, onion rings – you name it. Then drizzle all over with oil, vinegar and some salt and pepper, toss and serve – delicious!

PASTA AND BROAD BEAN SALAD

Serves 4

Ingredients	Metric	Imperial	American
Pasta shapes	175 g	6 oz	6 oz
Oil	45 ml	3 tbsp	3 tbsp
Vinegar	15 ml	1 tbsp	1 tbsp
Mayonnaise	30 ml	2 tbsp	2 tbsp
Chilli powder or cayenne to taste			
Salt and pepper			
Can of broad (lima) beans, drained	300 g	11 oz	1 small
Can of sweetcorn (corn), drained	200 g	7 oz	1 small

To serve: Lettuce

1. ook the pasta according to the packet directions. Drain and under rinse with cold water and drain again.

2. Mix together the oil, vinegar, mayonnaise, chilli powder or cayenne and a little salt and pepper in a bowl. Add the beans, sweetcorn and pasta and toss well together until pasta in the dressing

3. Serve with lettuce.

Preparation time: nil
Cooking time: about 12 minutes

CHEESE- AND EGG-BASED DISHES

Cheese and eggs are great forms of protein and, of course, they are very versatile. Cheese is not as cheap as it used to be but there are always good deals to be had in supermarkets. Edam is cheaper than Cheddar but some varieties don't melt in the same way. Use it if you prefer.

TIP: Buy a strong cheese because you don't need as much of it to get a good flavour. So taste as you add it to a sauce, for instance, and if you've got a cheesy enough taste, save the rest for another meal. Many of the mild ones taste like soap and you could add them for ever and never get a good flavour!

CHEESE AND VEGETABLE SOUP

For a tasty alternative use crumbled blue cheese instead of
Cheddar and leeks instead of onions – but make sure you
wash them really well as they often contain lots of grit.

Serves 4

Ingredients	Metric	Imperial	American
Carrots, chopped	2	2	2
Onions, chopped	2	2	2
Potatoes, chopped	3	3	3
Vegetable stock, made with 1 stock cube	600 ml	1 pt	2½ cups
Strong Cheddar cheese, grated	100 g	4 oz	1 cup
Milk	300 ml	½ pt	1¼ cups
Salt and pepper			
Dried mixed herbs	2.5 ml	½ tsp	½ tsp
To serve: Crusty bread			

1. Put the vegetables with the stock in a large saucepan.

2. Bring to the boil, reduce the heat, part-cover and simmer for about 15 minutes until really soft.

3. Mash with a potato masher, then stir in the cheese, milk and seasonings to taste. Heat through, stirring until the cheese melts.

4. Serve with lots of crusty bread.

Preparation time: 10 minutes
Cooking time: 20 minutes

SARNIES IN A BLANKET

Serves 2–4

Ingredients	Metric	Imperial	American
Slices of bread, spread with a little margarine	6	6	6
Marmite (Vegemite)			
Cheddar cheese, grated	100 g	4 oz	1 cup
Tomatoes, sliced	3	3	3
Eggs	3	3	3
Milk	300 ml	½ pt	1¼ cups
Salt and pepper			
Dried mixed herbs	2.5 ml	½ tsp	½ tsp
To serve: Green beans			

1. **Make up sandwiches using the bread and margarine, Marmite, three-quarters of the cheese and the tomatoes. Cut each round into 4.**

2. **Arrange in the base of a shallow, ovenproof dish.**

3. **Beat together the eggs, milk, a little salt and pepper and the herbs and pour over the sandwiches. Sprinkle with the remaining cheese.**

4. **Bake in a preheated oven at 190°C/375°F/gas mark 5 for about 40 minutes until golden brown and set.**

5. **Serve with green beans.**

Preparation time: 5 minutes
Cooking time: 40 minutes

CAULIFLOWER CHEESE

If you want to make a smaller version, halve the quantities
and use the rest of the cauliflower for any recipe that calls
for either a small cauli or for mixed vegetables.

Serves 4

Ingredients	Metric	Imperial	American
Cauliflower, cut into florets	1	1	1
Plain (all-purpose) flour	40 g	1½ oz	⅓ cup
Milk	600 ml	1 pt	2½ cups
Knob of margarine			
Dried mixed herbs	5 ml	1 tsp	1 tsp
Made mustard	5 ml	1 tsp	1 tsp
Salt and pepper			
Cheddar cheese, grated	175 g	6 oz	1½ cups
Handfuls of cornflakes or branflakes, crushed	2	2	2
To serve: Can of tomatoes			

1. Cook the cauliflower in boiling, salted water in a flameproof casserole (Dutch oven) until just tender – about 8 minutes, depending on the size of the florets. Drain in a colander.

2. Whisk the flour and milk together in the same casserole until smooth. Add the margarine. Bring to the boil and cook for 2 minutes, whisking all the time until smooth and thickened.

3. Stir in the herbs, mustard and a little salt and pepper. Add three-quarters of the cheese. Fold in the cauliflower.

4. Mix the remaining cheese with the crushed cereal and sprinkle over. Bake in a preheated oven at 200°C/400°F/ gas mark 6 for 20 minutes until golden on top.

5. Serve with tomatoes.

Preparation time: 5 minutes
Cooking time: 30 minutes

CURRIED CHEESE AND CORN GRILL

Serves 2

Ingredients	Metric	Imperial	American
Plain (all-purpose) flour	45 ml	3 tbsp	3 tbsp
Milk	300 ml	½ pt	1¼ cups
Knob of margarine			
Salt and pepper			
Cheddar cheese, grated	100 g	4 oz	1 cup
Can of sweetcorn (corn), drained	200 g	7 oz	1 small
Can of mixed pulses, drained	425 g	15 oz	1 large
Curry powder or paste	5 ml	1 tsp	1 tsp
Chilli powder (optional)	1.5 ml	¼ tsp	¼ tsp

To serve: Broccoli and toast

1. Whisk the flour and milk together in a flameproof casserole (Dutch oven). Add the margarine, bring to the boil and cook for 2 minutes, whisking all the time. Season to taste and stir in half the cheese.

2. Add the drained sweetcorn and pulses, the curry powder and chilli, if using. Heat through, stirring.

3. Sprinkle with the remaining cheese and place under a hot grill (broiler) until golden and bubbling

4. Serve hot with broccoli and toast.

Preparation time: 5 minutes
Cooking time: 10 minutes

GREEK FETA SALAD

Serves 2

Ingredients	Metric	Imperial	American
Small crisp lettuce, shredded	½	½	½
Tomatoes, cut into chunks	2	2	2
Piece of cucumber, cut into chunks	2.5 cm	1 in	1 in
Small onion, sliced and separated into rings	1	1	1
Feta cheese, cubed or crumbled	100 g	4 oz	1 cup
A few olives (optional)			
Pine nuts (optional)	30 ml	2 tbsp	2 tbsp
A little oil			
A little vinegar			
Salt and pepper			
Dried mixed herbs or basil	2.5 ml	½ tsp	½ tsp
To serve: Warm bread			

1. Put the lettuce in 2 shallow bowls. Top with the tomatoes, cucumber, onions and then the cheese. Scatter the olives and pine nuts (if using) over the top.

2. Drizzle with a little oil and vinegar, sprinkle very lightly with salt and add lots of pepper. Sprinkle with the herbs.

3. Serve with lots of warm bread.

Preparation time: 10 minutes
Cooking time: nil

ONION AND APPLE GRATIN

Serves 2–4

Ingredients	Metric	Imperial	American
Eating (dessert) apples, sliced	3–4	3–4	3–4
Onions, sliced	2	2	2
Dried sage or mixed herbs	5 ml	1 tsp	1 tsp
Salt and pepper			
Plain (all-purpose) flour	50 g	2 oz	¼ cup
Soft margarine	25 g	1 oz	2 tbsp
Cheddar cheese, grated	50 g	2 oz	½ cup

1. Layer the apples and onions in an ovenproof dish, seasoning with the sage or mixed herbs and a little salt and pepper.

2. Put the flour in a bowl. Add the margarine and, using a fork, mash it into the flour until the mixture resembles breadcrumbs. Stir in the cheese.

3. Scatter all over the onions and apples and bake in a preheated oven at 200°C/400°F/gas mark 6 for 30–40 minutes until the filling is soft and the top is golden brown.

Preparation time: 10 minutes
Cooking time: 40 minutes

OVEN OMELETTE

Serves 2–4

Ingredients	Metric	Imperial	American
Eggs, beaten	4	4	4
Carton of cottage cheese	250 g	9 oz	1 large
Milk	150 ml	¼ pt	⅔ cup
Salt and pepper			
Can of sweetcorn (corn), drained	200 g	7 oz	1 small
Small onion, chopped OR dried chives	1 10 ml	1 2 tsp	1 2 tsp
Dried mixed herbs	2.5 ml	½ tsp	½ tsp

To serve: Crusty bread and salad

1. **Mix all the ingredients in a large bowl.**

2. **Pour into a well greased ovenproof dish.**

3. **Bake in a preheated oven at 200°C/400°F/gas mark 6 for about 20 minutes until brown and firm.**

4. **Serve with crusty bread and salad.**

Preparation time: 5 minutes
Cooking time: 20 minutes

WELSH EGGS

Serves 2

Ingredients	Metric	Imperial	American
Margarine	75 g	3 oz	⅓ cup
Leeks, very well washed and sliced	450 g	1 lb	1 lb
Vegetable stock, made with 1 stock cube	300 ml	½ pt	1¼ cups
Dried milk powder (non-fat dry milk)	30 ml	2 tbsp	2 tbsp
Plain (all-purpose) flour	20 g	¾ oz	3 tbsp
Water	60 ml	4 tbsp	4 tbsp
Salt and pepper			
Eggs	4	4	4
To serve: Toast			

1. Melt the margarine in a saucepan. Add the leeks and cook, stirring, for 2 minutes.

2. Stir in the stock, bring to the boil, reduce the heat, part-cover and simmer for 10 minutes or until the leeks are tender.

3. Blend the milk powder, flour and water together to a smooth cream. Stir into the leeks and cook, stirring, for 2 minutes until thickened and smooth. Season to taste.

4. Meanwhile, hard-boil (hard-cook) the eggs (see page 12). Drain and plunge quickly into cold water. Shell and cut into halves.

5. Put the eggs in 2 warm shallow bowls and spoon the leek sauce over the top.

6. Serve with lots of toast.

Preparation time: 5 minutes
Cooking time: 12 minutes

STUFFED PANCAKES

Make these and serve with any of the savoury fillings,
suggested below; or use for dessert (see page 147–9).

Makes 8

Ingredients	Metric	Imperial	American
Plain (all-purpose) four	100 g	4 oz	1 cup
Pinch of salt			
Eggs	2	2	2
Milk and water mixed	300 ml	½ pt	1¼ cups
Oil for frying			

1. Put the flour and salt in a bowl.

2. Break in the eggs (break them into a cup first if you're
   not a dab hand at it!).

3. Add half the milk and water and beat with a balloon
   whisk until smooth. Stir in the remaining milk and water.

4. Heat a very little oil in a frying pan (skillet) until
   smoking. Pour off the excess into a cup to use for the
   next pancake. Add about 45 ml/3 tbsp batter – or
   enough to form a thin coat over the base of the pan
   when tilted round.

5. Cook over a moderate heat until the pancake is set and
   the base is golden. Flip over with a fish slice (or toss if
   you dare). Cook the other side briefly, then slide on to a
   plate over a pan of simmering water to keep it warm
   while cooking the remainder.

6. To serve: spread a little filling on each pancake, roll up and eat; or to be flash, fill, pack into a shallow ovenproof dish, dot with a little margarine or sprinkle with some grated cheese and heat through in a preheated oven at 190°C/375°F/gas mark 5 for about 20 minutes until piping hot and the top is sizzling.

 Preparation time: 5 minutes
Cooking time: about 4 minutes per pancake plus filling

TIP: If you don't want to eat all the pancakes in one go, wrap in foil and store in the fridge for up to 3 days or freeze for future use. Simply allow to thaw and use as required.

Suggested speedy fillings:

★ Ratatouille and cheese: Heat 1 425 g/15 oz/large can of ratatouille, spread over the pancakes and sprinkle with grated cheese (Mozzarella is a delicious change from Cheddar) before rolling up.

★ Baked bean and cheese: Heat 1 400g/14 oz/large can of baked beans, spread over the pancakes, sprinkle with grated cheese and roll up. Heat through if liked.

★ Spinach and cottage cheese: Cook 225 g/8 oz of frozen spinach according to the packet directions. Drain off any excess water. Stir in 1 250 g/9 oz/large carton of cottage cheese, heat through and season well, adding a little grated nutmeg if liked. Spread on the pancakes and roll up. Heat through if preferred.

★ French cheese and tomato: Slice a small Camembert cheese, lay on a flat pancake and top with a second one. Heat through before serving.

★ **Egg and cheese:** Top each pancake with some thin slices of cheese and a poached or fried egg. Fold over, rather than roll, the edges of the pancake before serving.

★ **Chilli bean pancakes:** Mash 1 425 g/15 oz/large can of drained red kidney beans with 60 ml/4 tbsp of tomato ketchup (catsup) and chilli powder to taste. Add a squeeze of garlic purée (paste) if you like. Moisten, if necessary, with water. Fill the pancakes with the mixture. Roll up, sprinkle with grated cheese and heat through before serving.

★ **Chinese-style:** Fill with any reheated leftover stir-fry and sprinkle with extra soy sauce.

TORTILLA

Serves 2

Ingredients	Metric	Imperial	American
Large potato, diced	1	1	1
Large onion, sliced	1	1	1
Oil	15 ml	1 tbsp	1 tbsp
Dried chives (optional)	5 ml	1 tsp	1 tsp
Eggs	4	4	4
Milk	30 ml	2 tbsp	2 tbsp
Salt and pepper			

To serve: Crusty bread and a salad

1. Put the potato and onion in a large frying pan (skillet) with the oil. Fry (sauté) for 4–5 minutes, stirring, until the vegetables are almost tender. Sprinkle the chives over, if using.

2. Break the eggs into a bowl and whisk in the milk and some salt and pepper. Pour into the pan and cook, lifting and stirring, until almost set.

3. Place the frying pan under a hot grill (broiler) until the top is golden brown and set.

4. Serve cut in wedges with crusty bread and salad.

Preparation time: 5 minutes
Cooking time: 10 minutes

EGG AND MUSHROOM PIE

Serves 2

Ingredients	Metric	Imperial	American
Potatoes, cut into even-sized pieces	450 g	1 lb	1 lb
Eggs, scrubbed under the cold tap	4	4	4
Knob of margarine			
Milk	15 ml	1 tbsp	1 tbsp
Can of condensed mushroom soup	295 g	10½ oz	1 small
Dried mixed herbs	2.5 ml	½ tsp	½ tsp
Cheddar cheese, grated	30 ml	2 tbsp	2 tbsp

To serve: Broccoli

1. Cook the potatoes and eggs (in their shells) in slightly salted, boiling water for 10–15 minutes until the potatoes are tender. Plunge the eggs into cold water. Shell, then roughly chop. Drain and mash the potatoes with the margarine and milk.

2. Heat the soup in a flameproof casserole (Dutch oven). Fold in the eggs, sprinkle with the herbs and cover with the mashed potatoes.

3. Sprinkle over the grated cheese and bake in a preheated oven at 200°C/400°F/gas mark 6 for about 15 minutes until the top is turning golden.

4. Serve hot with broccoli.

Preparation time: 10–15 minutes
Cooking time: 15 minutes

EGG AND POTATO SALAD

Serves 2

Ingredients	Metric	Imperial	American
New potatoes, scrubbed and cut into bite-sized pieces	450 g	1 lb	1 lb
Eggs, scrubbed under the cold tap	2	2	2
Mayonnaise	15 ml	1 tbsp	1 tbsp
Vinegar	5 ml	1 tsp	1 tsp
Dried mint or chives	5 ml	1 tsp	1 tsp
Salt and pepper			
Lettuce leaves			
Tomatoes, sliced	2	2	2

1. Put the potatoes and eggs (in their shells) in a saucepan of lightly salted water. Bring to the boil and boil until the potatoes are tender. Take the eggs out after 10 minutes (whether or not the potatoes are cooked) and plunge into cold water. Drain the potatoes when cooked and leave to cool.

2. Mix the mayonnaise, vinegar, herbs and a little salt and pepper together. Add the potatoes.

3. Shell the eggs and roughly chop. Add to the bowl and mix together gently but thoroughly. Preferably chill for several hours to allow the flavours to develop. Then spoon on to lettuce leaves and add the slices of tomato.

Preparation time: 10 minutes plus chilling
Cooking time: 10 minutes

Make a batch of any of the following before you have to get
stuck into revising or serious exam schedules. Then you'll have
something highly comforting and packed with goodness to give you
extra energy any time of the day or night. They're ideal to nibble
when you're feeling low or shattered or you've skipped a meal
like breakfast when you've overslept from all that studying ...
or whatever!. None of them takes long to make and they are
all far cheaper than buying equivalent bars in the supermarket
or health food shop.

WALNUT BROWNIES

Makes about 15

Ingredients	Metric	Imperial	American
Margarine	75 g	3 oz	⅓ cup
Carob or chocolate chips	50 g	2 oz	½ cup
Light brown sugar	175 g	6 oz	¾ cup
Instant coffee powder or granules	2.5 ml	½ tsp	½ tsp
Eggs, beaten	2	2	2
Walnut pieces, chopped	75 g	3 oz	¾ cup
Plain (all-purpose) or wholemeal flour	50 g	2 oz	½ cup
Baking powder	1.5 ml	¼ tsp	¼ tsp
Salt	1.5 ml	¼ tsp	¼ tsp

I. Melt the margarine, carob or chocolate chips, sugar and coffee in a saucepan, stirring.

2. Remove from the heat and stir in the remaining ingredients.

3. Turn into a greased 18 × 28 cm/7 × 11 in baking tin (pan). Bake in a preheated oven at 180°C/350°F/gas mark 4 for 35 minutes until the mixture springs back when lightly pressed.

4. Cool in the tin, then cut into squares and store in an airtight tin.

Preparation time: 10 minutes plus chilling
Cooking time: 10 minutes

BANANA SULTANA FLAPJACKS

Makes 16

Ingredients	Metric	Imperial	American
Soft margarine	75 g	3 oz	⅓ cup
Light brown sugar	100 g	4 oz	½ cup
Golden (light corn) syrup or honey	15 ml	1 tbsp	1 tbsp
Large, ripe banana, mashed	1	1	1
Sultanas (golden raisins) or raisins	50 g	2 oz	⅓ cup
Porridge oats	275 g	10 oz	2½ cups

1. Put the margarine, sugar and syrup or honey in a bowl and beat with a wooden spoon until smooth and fluffy.

2. Stir in the remaining ingredients and press into a greased 18 × 28 cm/7 × 11 in baking tin (pan).

3. Bake in a preheated oven at 180°C/350°F/gas mark 4 for about 30 minutes or until golden brown.

4. Leave to cool for 10 minutes, then mark into fingers with the back of a knife. Leave until completely cold before cutting up. Store in an airtight tin.

Preparation time: 5 minutes
Cooking time: 30 minutes

CAROB NIBBLES

Use cocoa (unsweetened chocolate) powder
instead of carob if you prefer.

Makes about 14

Ingredients	Metric	Imperial	American
Light brown sugar	50 g	2 oz	¼ cup
Golden (light corn) syrup or honey	30 ml	2 tbsp	2 tbsp
Margarine	75 g	3 oz	⅓ cup
Porridge oats	225 g	8 oz	2 cups
Chopped mixed nuts	25 g	1 oz	¼ cup
Chopped dates or raisins	50 g	2 oz	⅓ cup
Carob powder	45 ml	3 tbsp	3 tbsp

1. Put the sugar, syrup or honey and margarine in a large saucepan and heat until melted.

2. Stir in the remaining ingredients and mix well.

3. Press into a large, greased, shallow baking tin (pan), cover with foil or clingfilm (plastic wrap) and chill for at least 3 hours to set.

4. Cut into squares. Store in an airtight container.

Preparation time: nil
Cooking time: 10 minutes plus chilling

CHEWY FRUIT SALAD BARS

Makes 15

Ingredients	Metric	Imperial	American
Can of evaporated milk	175 g	6 oz	1 small
Honey	20 ml	4 tsp	4 tsp
Orange or apple juice	45 ml	3 tbsp	3 tbsp
Margarine	50 g	2 oz	¼ cup
Light brown sugar	50 g	2 oz	¼ cup
Dried fruit salad, chopped, discarding any stones (pits)	225 g	8 oz	1 pkt
Desiccated (shredded) coconut	100 g	4 oz	1 cup
Porridge oats	225 g	8 oz	2 cups

1. Heat the evaporated milk with the honey, juice, margarine and sugar until melted.

2. Stir in the remaining ingredients and mix well.

3. Press into a greased 18 × 28 cm/7 × 11 in shallow baking tin (pan). Cover with foil or clingfilm (plastic wrap) and chill overnight until firm.

4. Cut into bars and store in an airtight container.

Preparation time: nil
Cooking time: 10 minutes plus chilling

NO-BAKE CRUNCHY BARS

Makes 12–16

Ingredients	Metric	Imperial	American
Margarine	175 g	6 oz	¾ cup
Light brown sugar	50 g	2 oz	¼ cup
Golden (light corn) syrup or honey	30 ml	2 tbsp	2 tbsp
Carob or cocoa (unsweetened chocolate) powder	45 ml	3 tbsp	3 tbsp
Raisins	75 g	3 oz	½ cup
Original Oat Crunch Cereal (supermarket own brands are cheapest)	350 g	12 oz	3 cups
Carob or plain (semi-sweet) chocolate bar	225 g	8 oz	8 oz

1. Melt the margarine, sugar and syrup or honey in a pan and stir in the carob or cocoa powder, raisins and cereal.

2. Press into a greased 18 × 28 cm/7 × 11 in shallow baking tin (pan).

3. Melt the carob or chocolate bar in a bowl over a pan of hot water. (If you do it straight into a saucepan it is likely to burn.) Spread thinly over the cereal mixture, right to the corners. Chill until set.

4. Cut in fingers and store in an airtight tin.

Preparation time: nil
Cooking time: 10 minutes plus chilling

Most students live off yoghurts or fresh fruit for afters which is a great idea. But every now and then you might hanker after a real pud – something sweet and luscious but still good for you. Here are some really simple ideas which taste terrific and are ideal for filling up on – especially when you have people round to share them with.

BREAD PUD

Makes about 12 squares

Ingredients	Metric	Imperial	American
Milk	300 ml	½ pt	1¼ cups
Pinch of salt			
Margarine	50 g	2 oz	¼ cup
Slices of bread, cubed	8	8	8
Eggs, beaten	2	2	2
Mixed dried (cake) fruit	175 g	6 oz	1 cup
Light brown sugar	40 g	1½ oz	3 tbsp
Mixed (apple pie) spice or cinnamon	5 ml	1 tsp	1 tsp
A little caster (superfine) sugar			

1. Put the milk, salt and margarine in a large saucepan and bring to the boil. Remove from the heat.

2. Add the bread and leave to stand for 15 minutes.

3. Add the remaining ingredients except the caster sugar and mix well. Turn into a greased baking tin (pan) and bake in a preheated oven at 180°C/350°F/gas mark 4 for about 45 minutes until lightly browned and set.

4. Sprinkle with caster sugar and serve hot or cold, cut into squares.

Preparation time: 10 minutes plus standing
Cooking time: 45 minutes

PINEAPPLE LOAF

Serves 4–5

Ingredients	Metric	Imperial	American
Plain (all-purpose) flour	350 g	12 oz	3 cups
Baking powder	15 ml	1 tbsp	1 tbsp
Bicarbonate of soda (baking soda)	2.5 ml	½ tsp	½ tsp
Light brown sugar	100 g	4 oz	½ cup
Soft margarine	150 g	5 oz	⅔ cup
Eggs, beaten	3	3	3
Milk	30 ml	2 tbsp	2 tbsp
Ground cinnamon	5 ml	1 tsp	1 tsp
Honey	30 ml	2 tbsp	2 tbsp
Can of pineapple rings, drained, the fruit chopped and the juice reserved	225 g	8 oz	1 small

Put all the ingredients in a large bowl and beat together well.

Turn into a greased 450 g/1 lb loaf tin (pan) or baking dish and bake on a low shelf in a preheated oven at 180°C/350°F/gas mark 4 for about 1 hour or until firm to the touch. Leave to cool for a few minutes. Loosen the edges and turn out.

3. Serve warm or cold with the reserved juice, if liked.

Preparation time: 5 minutes
Cooking time: 1 hour

SWEET PANCAKES

Serves 4

Ingredients	Metric	Imperial	American
1 quantity of pancake mix [see Stuffed Pancakes page 132]			
Caster (superfine) sugar			
Lemon juice OR any flavour jam, warmed			

I. Make the pancakes according to the directions on page 132.

2. Either sprinkle with sugar and lemon juice OR spread with a little warm jam. Roll up and serve.

Preparation time: 5 minutes
Cooking time: about 4 minutes per pancake

CHOCOLATE NUT CREPES

Serves 4

Ingredients	Metric	Imperial	American
1 quantity of pancake mix [see Stuffed Pancakes page 132]			
Chocolate hazelnut spread			
Chopped mixed nuts	50 g	2 oz	½ cup
Crème fraîche	150 ml	¼ pt	⅔ cup

I. **Make up the pancakes according to the directions on page 132.**

2. **Spread each with a little chocolate hazelnut spread, sprinkle with a few nuts and roll up. Serve with a dollop of crème fraîche on top of each portion.**

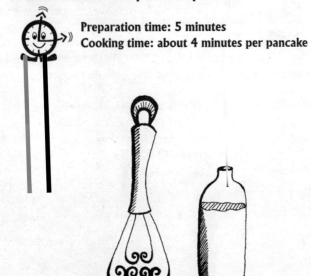

Preparation time: 5 minutes
Cooking time: about 4 minutes per pancake

PEAR CLAFOUTIE

Serves 4

Ingredients	Metric	Imperial	American
Can of pear quarters, drained, reserving the juice	420 g	15 oz	1 large
1 quantity of pancake mix (see Stuffed Pancakes page 132)			
Nuts (e.g. flaked almonds, chopped mix or chopped walnuts)	25 g	1 oz	¼ cup
Caster (superfine) sugar			
To serve: Custard			

1. Arrange the pears in the base of a greased, shallow, ovenproof dish.

2. Make up the pancake mix and pour over. Sprinkle with nuts.

3. Bake in a preheated oven at 200°C/400°F/gas mark 6 for about 30 minutes until risen and golden brown.

4. Dust with caster sugar before serving with custard.

Preparation time: 10 minutes
Cooking time: 30 minutes

NO-FUSS FRUIT CRUMBLE

Serves 4

Ingredients	Metric	Imperial	American
Can of fruit, drained, reserving the juice	410 g	14½ oz	1 large
Weetabix	2	2	2
Light brown sugar	15 ml	1 tbsp	1 tbsp
Margarine, melted	50 g	2 oz	¼ cup
Ground ginger, cinnamon or mixed (apple pie) spice	2.5 ml	½ tsp	½ tsp
To serve: Yoghurt OR custard			

1. Put the fruit in an ovenproof dish.

2. Crumble the Weetabix and mix with the sugar and melted margarine. Add the spice. Sprinkle over the fruit, pressing down lightly.

3. Bake in a preheated oven at 190°C/375°F/gas mark 5 for about 15 minutes until the top is crisp.

4. Serve hot with yoghurt or custard.

Preparation time: 5 minutes
Cooking time: 15 minutes

TROPICAL SUNDAE

Serves 4

Ingredients	Metric	Imperial	American
Fresh or dried dates, stoned (pitted) and chopped	12	12	12
Large bananas, sliced	2	2	2
Can of pineapple in natural juice, chopped	225 g	8 oz	1 small
Crème fraîche or plain yoghurt	150 ml	¼ pt	⅔ cup

Mix the fruits together with the pineapple juice and spoon into 4 glasses. Top with crème fraîche and serve.

Preparation time: 5 minutes
Cooking time: nil

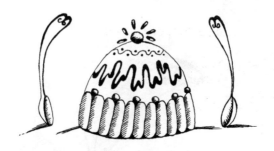

CHUNKY FRUIT FOOL

Serves 4

Ingredients	Metric	Imperial	American
Can of apricots (or other fruit) in natural juice, drained, reserving the juice	410 g	14½ oz	1 large
Can of custard	400 g	14 oz	1 large
Thick plain yoghurt	150 ml	¼ pt	⅔ cup

I. **Mash the fruit well with a fork.**

2. **Stir in the custard, then fold in the yoghurt.**

3. **Spoon into glasses.**

4. **Serve chilled with the juice poured over at the last minute.**

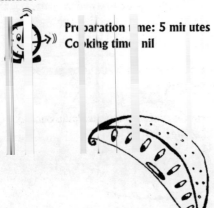

Preparation time: 5 minutes
Cooking time: nil

ORANGE TRIFLE

Serves 4

Ingredients	Metric	Imperial	American
Jam Swiss (jelly) roll, sliced	1	1	1
Can of broken mandarin segments	300 g	11 oz	1 small
Packet of orange-flavoured vegetarian jelly (jello)	1	1	1
Can of custard, chilled	400 g	14 oz	1 large
Grated chocolate or carob			

1. Put the Swiss roll slices in the base of a serving dish.

2. Drain the mandarin pieces, reserving the juice. Scatter the fruit over the Swiss roll.

3. Make up the jelly using the juice instead of some of the water. Cool slightly, then pour over the sponge and fruit and chill until set.

4. Spoon the custard over and sprinkle with grated chocolate before serving.

Preparation time: 10 minutes plus cooling
Cooking time: nil

RASPBERRY QUARK LAYER DESSERT

Serves 4

Ingredients	Metric	Imperial	American
Can of raspberries	300 g	11 oz	1 small
Packet of raspberry-flavoured vegetarian jelly (jello)	1	1	1
Quark	100 g	4 oz	½ cup

1. Make up the raspberries and their juice to 600 ml/1pt/ 2½ cups with water. Use a little to dissolve the jelly, then stir in the remainder.

2. Whisk in the quark, then pour into a serving dish. The mixture will separate as it cools. Chill until set.

Preparation time: 10 minutes plus chilling
Cooking time: nil

INSTANT CHEESECAKES

Serves 4

Ingredients	Metric	Imperial	American
Slices of slab sponge cake	4	4	4
Soft fruits in season (e.g. strawberries, raspberries or blackberries)	225 g	8 oz	8 oz
Low-fat soft cheese	225 g	8 oz	1 cup
Caster (superfine) sugar	15 ml	1 tbsp	1 tbsp

1. Put the slices of cake into 4 serving dishes.

2. Mash the fruits, reserving 4 whole ones (or halved strawberries) for decoration.

3. Stir in the cheese and sugar and mix well.

4. Pile on the cake and top each with a berry. Chill until ready to serve.

Preparation time: 10 minutes plus chilling
Cooking time: nil

JAMAICAN LAYER CAKE

Serves 4–6

Ingredients	Metric	Imperial	American
Slab Jamaican ginger cake	1	1	1
Bananas	2	2	2
Lemon juice	5 ml	1 tsp	1 tsp
Crème fraîche	150 ml	¼ pt	⅔ cup
Grated chocolate			

1. Cut the cake lengthways into 3 slices.

2. Mash the bananas with the lemon juice and use to sandwich the layers back together again.

3. Gently spread the crème fraîche over the top and sprinkle with a little grated chocolate.

4. Chill before serving, cut into slices (the tricky bit!).

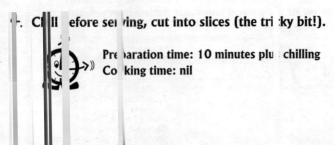

Preparation time: 10 minutes plus chilling
Cooking time: nil

INDEX

FEED ME

INDEX

159

THE NEW STUDENTS' VEGGIE COOKBOOK